HAMPSHIRE MURDERS

HAMPSHIRE
Murders

Roger Guttridge

Ensign
PUBLICATIONS

First published in Great Britain by Ensign Publications, 2 Redcar Street, Southampton SO1 5LL

Copyright © Roger Guttridge 1990

Publisher: David Graves
Editors: Roy Gasson Associates
Typeset: PageMerger, Southampton

Printed and bound in Great Britain by Bell & Bain Ltd., Thornliebank, Glasgow

British Library Cataloguing in Publication Data
Guttridge, Roger 1950–
Hampshire murders.
1. Hampshire. Murder, history
I. Title
364.1'523'094227

ISBN 1 85455 022 5

CONTENTS

1

THE HUSBAND KILLERS

Domestic murders in fact and fiction

People came from far and wide for the public execution of Lady Kirk. By foot, by horse and by carriage they travelled, an estimated 10,000 souls converging on Winchester Common to witness the death throes of a mass murderess. This was no ordinary execution, neither was the central character an ordinary criminal or her crimes ordinary crimes. She was a member of the landed classes, a woman of the utmost respectability to whom the rest of society looked up in awe. And her crimes were of a particularly heinous variety, involving the deliberate poisoning not only of her two sons and one of her two daughters but also of her husband, a man well known for his service to God and his generosity to the poor.

It was an extraordinary set of circumstances and one that meant an even more dramatic spectacle than usual for those for whom a "hang fair" was a not infrequent source of entertainment. For the murder of a man by his wife was thought by the law-makers of old England to deserve a more severe penalty than most other forms of murder, including the murder of a wife by her husband. "Run-of-the-mill" murderers faced straightforward hanging with, at worst, the quartering and public display of their corpses after death. But women who murdered their husbands were guilty not simply of murder but of "petty treason", for which the punishment was to be publicly burned at the stake. Many unfortunate English women went to their deaths in this way, victims of a law that remained on the statute book until 1828, though it had in practice lapsed before the end of the 18th century. Most women were spared the full ordeal of being burned alive, for they were usually garrotted at the stake by an executioner before the fire reached them. But there were exceptions, including the unfortunate Catherine Hayes, burned at Tyburn in 1726, whose executioner fled the advancing flames before he had completed his dreadful work. As the screaming woman struggled to kick away the burning faggots, he dropped the rope and ran. Other faggots were immediately heaped upon her, but she survived amid the flames for a considerable time.

Exactly how Lady Kirk was put to death is not clear, but the only contemporary description of the event yet discovered speaks of her being "burnt to death that very day". That in itself must have been a satisfying sight for the bloodthirsty audience but there was also an unexpected bonus. As the flames took hold, Lady Kirk's only surviving daughter thrust a letter into the hands of a priest who stood among the spectators and rushed towards the pyre. Then, to the astonishment of the crowd, she threw herself into the flames and, "with dismal shrieks and cries", was consumed along with her mother.

The Rev. Mr Jones opened the letter.

"Let this be published as a warning to all others not to prove false in love for the sake of gold, which has been my ruin," the young woman had written. "For one James Parker, whom I prized above my soul, to get my father's estate into my own hands that I might have him for my husband, I poisoned my father, two brothers and a sister, and to save myself I swore against my mother falsely, and have taken her life wrongfully, a sure way to the utter destruction of my soul. And, sir, let this my desire be published, that young people may take warning."

The warning was indeed published, in the form of a pamphlet, *A True and Genuine Account of Lady Kirk, Who was Tried at the Assizes at Winchester in Hampshire and found Guilty of Poisoning her Husband, Two Sons and a Daughter.* After summarizing the drama of the execution and quoting the daughter's letter, the pamphlet goes on to recount the whole sorry tale in verse. It tells of Lord Kirk's inheritance of an estate worth £1,600 a year, of his charitable deeds and his kindness to the poor, of his "virtuous wife", two sons, and "two daughters fair". It also tells that the younger daughter was doted upon by her parents – and that it was this that "their ruin did begin". The verse continues:

> This maid had suitors far and near,
> But none could then obtain her love;

At last a grocer's son did steer,
A'courting to this maiden fair.

He brought this maiden to consent,
With that he to her parents went,
To ask of them their good free will,
Which they poor souls did give consent.

He with a treacherous heart did say,
"Do get your father's estate for me",
With tears she said "I can't presume",
"Then fare thee well", replied he.

When he had left her all in woe,
She yielded to the devil's will,
Who soon did put her in a way,
These cruel murders to fulfill.

According to the verse, the misguided girl – determined to make herself a wealthy heiress, as James Parker demanded – travelled some miles from her home to buy poison. On her return she mixed it into a bowl of punch and, in her mother's absence, served it to the rest of her family. Next morning, her father, brothers, and sister were all found dead in their beds. A doctor was summoned, who pronounced that they had been poisoned. The daughter then said that she had seen her mother adding something to the punch bowl and accused her of the murder. Her story was, as we have seen, accepted by the court. The young man for whom she had killed committed suicide, after the burnings, by throwing himself into a well.

Such is the story, told in prose and verse, of Lady Kirk and her ill-fated family. It's a sorry tale indeed and one that must, at the time, have had a major impact on the community in which the tragic events unfolded. But what was that time? Where was that community? Who was the girl whose love for a grocer's son led to the deaths of her entire family and her young lover as well? The family's aristocratic background, coupled with their clearly stated association with Hampshire, should make such information relatively easy to discover. Surprisingly, this is not the case. The pamphlet is undated, but experts at the British Library have estimated its date of publication at about 1760. Yet a search of the Western Circuit Assize Court records, which included the Hampshire Assizes at Winchester, covering the period from 1737 until well into the 19th century, yielded no mention of any defendant called Lady Kirk. Nor did any gazetteer yield mention south of Yorkshire of "a town call'd Thirsk by name, near Winchester so fair" – the place where, according to the pamphlet, the Kirk family lived.

What, then, is the reality behind the story told in the pamphlet? Did the murders really happen in Hampshire? Did they involve a Hampshire family? Did they happen at all? Or were they the product of a vivid 18th century imagination?

A clue to the truth may lie in the observations of a 19th century Hampshire historian who, over the initials A.B., contributed in 1889 an article to the antiquarian magazine *Hampshire Notes and Queries*. A.B. describes a quite different pamphlet, or chapbook, *The Winchester Tragedy*. This purported to be "A true and particular account of a Cruel and Inhuman Murder, Committed on the Body of Mary Thomas, Near Winchester, in the County of Hants, by John Williams, A young Farmer in the same Neighbourhood on Sunday last". The story it relates is that Williams won the heart of his victim, a labourer's daughter, but afterwards abandoned her.

"Repeated meetings of criminality produced the usual consequences and the deluded girl found herself pregnant," says the chapbook, "with the addition to her misery, that where she expected the most comfort, she found the least, for John Williams not only evaded his promise, but entirely forsook her. She seldom saw him; and when she did, met with cold indifference and ill-treatment. Where he once loved he now hated; and was continually ruminating how to get rid of her and the infant in her womb. This cruel treatment of an unfortunate girl whom he had seduced was increased by his fixing his eyes on a farmer's daughter, whose uncle had left her £200, and he was determined, if possible, to obtain her hand."

Mary Thomas's misery was eased only when Williams finally wrote asking her to meet him, as he had "something very particular to propose to you, which may be of the greatest benefit to us". Encouraged and somewhat relieved, the 18-year-old girl kept the appointment and walked with her lover until he invited her to sit down on a bank. Then, putting his arms around Mary as if to kiss her, he drew a knife and cut her throat, throwing her body in a ditch and covering it with brambles. Despite the blood on his clothes and the letter of reply from Mary found in his possession, Williams denied the crime. But at the coroner's inquest, he was "desired to touch the body, which he did, when it bled at the nose. By this circumstance, he was so shocked that he was fully committed to take his trial at Hants Assizes."

The chapbook examined by A.B. bore no date but the type and style led him to conclude that it was printed in the mid-18th century. It contained four rough woodcuts and concluded with a "copy of verses to the Fair Sex", which were "of the usual ballad doggerel of the time". The printer's imprint was "J. Pitts, 1, Great Andrew-street, 7 Dials." But A.B. was suspicious.

"Is there a tradition in Winchester of a young woman having been murdered under these circumstances?" he asked. "For ourselves we strongly, from the absence of dates, suspect that the story, with the necessary changes of name and places, did service in various other counties."

A century later there is no reason to dispute A.B.'s conclusion. The British Library has other editions of the chapbook, which they believe date from about 1811. The wording of the tale appears to be identical and there are woodcuts, too. But different printers are named on the imprints and, as with the case of Lady Kirk, neither the Hampshire Assize lists nor the local newspapers for the relevant periods make mention of a murder trial involving a defendant called John Williams. A.B.'s suspicions about the document's authenticity were almost certainly justified; and so, in all probability, are our own doubts about the Lady Kirk saga.

Pamphlets like these were distributed by pedlars or chapmen around the towns and villages of 18th century England, often to the deception of the reading public. But the same doubts and suspicions would not be justified in every case. Many pamphlets, although they may impose a moralistic gloss upon their reporting, were factually accurate. One such is the *Full and True Account of a most Barbarous and Bloody Murther*, which gives an account of a murder at Romsey in 1686. The preciseness of the names, dates and other details suggests that the pamphlet is more reliable than those on Lady Kirk and John Williams.

The victim was publican William Ives, who kept an inn "at the sign of the Hatchet", where he lived with his wife, Esther, and their children. By 1686 the marriage was foundering, largely on account of Esther's flourishing friendship with another man. He was John Noyse, a cooper from the village of West Wellow, two miles from Romsey, described in the pamphlet as a "person of ill fame" and a "very dissolute liver". Of late Noyes had been "keeping company, in a more familiar manner than was convenient, with the wife of William Ives".

On the night of February 5, 1686, Noyes stayed drinking at the Hatchet until one or two in the morning and it was during this time that the Romsey bellman, who happened to be passing, heard William Ives cry out in a voice which sounded confused.

"What does thou do to me, Noyse?" Ives was heard to say.

Some time later, Esther Ives knocked up a neighbour to ask for a light for a candle. She also called at another alehouse, the Black Boy, "and there had called up the woman to have of her some strongwater, under pretence that her husband was very much indisposed".

Later still, the bellman went past the Hatchet again. This time he heard different sounds, those of children weeping and wailing. Being "much desirous to know the cause of the children's cries at so unseasonable a time", the bellman moved under the window of Ives's house and asked what was going on. In "mournful voices" the children replied that their father was dead. Their mother added that he had collapsed and died apparently of natural causes. Not satisfied with the explanation, the bellman hurried to inform the constable of the watch, who in turn fetched a guard and headed for the Hatchet.

"Upon their entering the house of Ives, and going upstairs, they found Noyse and Esther Ives the wife very busy about Ives, who was indeed dead, in dressing him, viz. putting on his breeches, stockings, shoes and other wearing apparel; having newly, as was supposed, taken him out of his bed, it being then warm, the design of which, as many imagined, and they in part confessed, was that being so clothed they would have tumbled him downstairs, that so the bruises thereby occasioned might colour the pretence they intended to make: that he accidentally and unfortunately fell down them and so consequently lost his life. But they being known to be people of bad conversations, the constable would not be so satisfied; but with the light he then had, proceeded to make a narrower inspection into the unhappy business: causing the dead body to be diligently searched, securing at the same time Noyes and Esther Ives, as suspecting the matter to be otherwise than they pretended, whose pretence then was that he died suddenly of some extraordinary distemper, at which they could not guess.

"But upon a narrow search of the body, much violence appeared to be done to the neck of the party deceased, either by strangling or twisting insomuch that the blood had issued from him in abundance, and stained the pillow whereon his head had lain, as also upon his shirt: and it further appeared that through the vehemency of his struggling and contending for life, his water had come from him, with which not only his shirt but part of the bed was wet."

Observing these "plain signs and palpable demonstrations of a murther", the constable and his companions decided to make a more thorough search of the two suspects, with the result that they found "much blood" upon Esther Ives, which they supposed had come from her husband either when she was "assistant to Noyse in perpetrating the wicked and unnatural murther" or when she was trying to move the body from the bed. Both were arrested and brought before a justice of the peace, who committed them to Romsey jail to await their trial at the Lent Assizes in Winchester. A coroner's inquest was also held, and a verdict of wilful murder returned.

The trial was held on February 24, 1686, and the prosecution contended that Noyse and Esther Ives had "conspired against Ives, murthered him by strangling or breaking his neck to make a freer way for their unlawful lust or, as it is conjectured, being rid of him they might marry". In his defence, Noyes claimed that he was in Ives' house when "a quarrel happened between the said Ives and his wife, and that all that he did on that occasion was only to interpose, that he might do the good office of parting them". But Esther Ives contradicted this story, declaring under oath that Noyse was the person who murdered her husband.

"The jury, after some consideration of the matter of fact, gave in their verdict, that John Noyse and Esther Ives were guilty of the wilful murther whereof they stood indicted, so that in the close of the Assize, they accordingly received sentence of death, viz. the former to be hanged and the latter to be burnt; and so returned to prison, in order to be executed according to the said sentences."

March 11 was the date appointed for the executions, and the couple were collected by the sheriffs officers from Winchester jail, where they had languished for some days to "bewail their wicked and barbarous act". They were then placed upon a single horse and taken back to Romsey, where the executions were to be carried out.

"John Noyse, turning to the spectators, who came to see him executed, desired them, especially the younger sort, above all things, not to profane the Sabbath day, but to keep it with all reverence and due regard; as likewise to refrain from drunkenness, which occasions so many evils and mischiefs in the world. He confessed he had long kept company with Esther Ives, in a lascivious and unlawful manner. After this and some other expressions, he went up the ladder, and when the rope was made fast, turned himself off; and about half-an-hour after, was cut down, in order to his interment or burial."

Esther Ives was a good deal less talkative. "Being brought to the stake, she said very little; but being fastened thereto, and the fuel placed about her, after the executioner had strangled her, the fire was kindled and she consumed to ashes."

Almost a hundred years after Esther Ives died at the stake, a Portsmouth woman, Mary Bailey, found herself facing a court that could condemn her to the same fate. Her situation was almost identical to that of Esther Ives as she stood in the dock at the Lent Assizes in 1884. Beside her was her lover John Quin, a private in the Portsmouth Division of Marines and, like herself, a native of Ireland. Together they stood accused of murdering Mary's husband, Cornelius Bailey.

"The unfortunate husband had for some time discovered an intimacy between his wife and Quin," reported the Hampshire Chronicle. "When he remonstrated with his wife upon the baseness of her conduct, she not only abused him in the grossest terms, but brought Quin home to their house in Warburton Street, Portsmouth, in open defiance of her husband, and they both joined in abusing, beating and ill-using him, until they perpetrated this unnatural murder."

Cornelius Bailey had already reported Quin to his officers, as a result of which a guard was despatched to remove him from the Bailey house and orders given for him to stay within the barracks and never to go back to the house again. But within four or five days he was back, and Bailey came home one day to find Quin and Mary at dinner together, having left nothing for him. Bailey's reaction was witnessed by a servant girl who was in the house at the time. "He was very angry," she recalled later, "and complained that it was very hard to be treated in that manner, and to have nothing to eat or drink, upon which his wife and Quin began abusing and beating him in a shocking manner."

The girl left the house at this point and did not return until 6 o'clock in the evening, at which time she found Quin and Mary "together below stairs", while Cornelius had gone to lie on the bed. The girl went upstairs and asked him what was the matter. He replied that his wife and Quin had "beat him unmercifully and used him very ill". His words were overheard by Mary, who immediately rushed up the stairs, closely followed by her lover. They then dragged Cornelius from the bed and across the room and kicked him down the stairs, telling the girl that it was no business of hers. The girl warned the couple that if they went on as they were they would end up murdering Bailey, to which Mary replied: "Then we'll have a sweet burying, hot rolls and treacle!"

Mary then went to her husband and feigned affection, saying: "My dear, though you are so cross to me, I am the best friend you have." Almost immediately she and Quin "fell upon him again, beating and kicking him in the most cruel manner". The girl ran into the street to call for help, which was immediately offered by a male passer-by. He went into the house and asked Mary and Quin what they had been doing, to which Mary replied that her husband was only troubled by a nosebleed and that nobody had hurt him. The man was not satisfied. He looked down at the floor, which was covered in blood.

XXXI.

A Full and True

ACCOUNT

OF A MOST

Barbarous and Bloody

MURTHER,

COMMITTED

By *Esther Ives*, with the Assistance of *John Noyse* a Cooper; on the Body of *William Ives*, her Husband, at *Rum-sey* in *Hampshire*, on the Fifth day of *February* 1686. Together with the Miraculous and Wonderful Discovery of the Murther and Murtherers.

AS ALSO

An Account of their TRYALS at the last Assizes, holden at *Winchester*, where being found guilty of the said Murther, they received Sentence of Death, *viz. John Noyse* to be Hang'd, and *Esther Ive* to be Burnt. With their manner of Behaviour and Execution, according to the said Sentence.

This may be Printed, R. P.

Printed for *P. Brooksby* at the *Golden Ball* in *Pye-corner.*

Title page of the broadsheet describing the murder of William Ives.

"Who has been using you ill?" he asked Bailey.

Bailey blamed his wife and Quin for his injuries, from which, he said, he feared he would die. Looking at him, the passer-by found it hard to disagree. Their fears were soon confirmed. A surgeon was called in, not to treat Bailey but to examine his dead body. He reported that "the deceased had every external mark of the most cruel and barbarous treatment" and that "upon opening the head he found it fractured from a violent blow on the temple, which occasioned his death".

Quin and Mary Bailey were tried for murder during the first week of March 1784 and the prosecution witnesses included a sergeant of Marines, the servant girl, the passer-by and the surgeon who examined Bailey's body. To avoid the charge of petty treason, Mary claimed that Cornelius Bailey was not her legal husband — but this statement was disputed by another witness, who claimed to have attended their wedding. Quin, in his defence, rather unconvincingly asserted that "the cruel treatment he had at different times received from the deceased was the only reason for his committing so rash an action".

The jury had little hesitation in pronouncing both defendants guilty and the judge, after describing the horrific and inhuman nature of the crime, passed the inevitable sentences. John Quin was to be hanged at Winchester on Monday March 8 and his body then delivered to a surgeon to be dissected and anatomized. Mary Bailey was to be drawn on a hurdle to the place of execution on the same date "and there burned with fire until she be dead".

The pair had less than a week to contemplate their fate and Winchester was soon buzzing with expectation. The executions were to be carried out at Gallows Hill, on the road to Andover and Newbury about a mile from Winchester city centre. Local boys were enlisted to haul faggots for the fire to the site — exciting work from which the youngsters derived much pleasure. At the appointed time and only a few yards from each other, Quin and Mary Bailey met their respective fates, the latter, despite the terminology of her sentence, being strangled before the fire reached her.

"The woman," reported the *Hampshire Chronicle*, "beheld the dreadful preparations for her untimely exit with a great appearance of undismay; and both of them protested the innocence of their intentions so far as respected his murder. Their behaviour on the whole was penitent and devout."

Mary Bailey was the last woman to be burned at the stake in Hampshire. The event became legendary and was recalled by generations of Winchester folk. More than sixty years later, part of the stake to which Mary was tied could still be seen, standing eighteen inches above the ground, by visitors to Gallows Hill.

Perhaps just a few of the 10,000 Hampshire ghouls who assembled at the same site in March 1819 may have noticed the fire-damaged, weather-worn stake, but most would have been wholly intent on the fun of another public execution. They were there to watch the hanging of 61-year-old Sarah Huntingford for the murder of her husband the previous autumn.

Sarah and her husband, Thomas, who was ten years older than her, had for the last five years occupied two rooms of a house in Orange Street, Portsea, where their landlady was a widow called Louisa Jennings. According to Mrs Jennings, the Huntingfords "appeared to live very happy and comfortable". They quarrelled occasionally, but their quarrels never developed to the point of violence. Sarah conducted herself "with great care and attention towards her husband, except when a little the worse for liquor". But she did often complain of giddiness in her head and memory loss and was afraid that she would one day "lose her senses".

In the view of shipwright Samuel Beatley, who also lodged with Mrs Jennings, both Sarah and Thomas Huntingford had been alcoholics for the last five years. He too had heard Mrs Huntingford complain of "pains in the head and want of recollection" and on many occasions he had known her to go out on an errand only to return later without whatever she had gone for. The poor woman had also lost one eye some years earlier, when she caught cold after lying in and developed an "inflammation in her head". But despite all these problems, her conduct towards her husband was, in Beatley's view, the "tenderest imaginable".

On the evening of October 23, 1818, everything appeared normal in the Orange Street household and relations between Thomas and Sarah seemed as good as ever. The couple's landlady supped with them in the front parlour and, as she was later to testify, both were sober and in good humour with each other. Mrs Jennings went to her own room at 8.45 and about half-an-hour later she heard the Huntingfords go upstairs, Thomas Huntingford calling out, "Good night, neighbour," as he passed her door.

At 3 o'clock the following morning Samuel Beatley was awoken by a noise "like someone coming downstairs harder than usual". He reached out from his bed to open the casement window and looked into the yard below. It was a moonlit night and he could see a woman walking to and fro across the yard, wringing her hands in great agitation. He called out, "Who is there?" There was no answer but the woman immediately turned and entered the house through the back door. Beatley dressed himself and on opening his door saw Mrs

Huntingford on the stairs, a candle in her hand. She appeared much alarmed and he asked her what was the matter. Her hands were shaking and she dropped the candle on the landing. Then she exclaimed: "I am murdered and robbed."

Beatley, who could see no signs of violence on Mrs Huntingford's person, called Mrs Jennings, who appeared almost immediately with another candle, from which the shipwright relit the one which the agitated woman had dropped. While this was going on, Mrs Huntingford kept repeating: "What shall I do? What shall I do?" She then continued up the stairs to her own room, closely followed by Mrs Jennings.

The landlady was shocked by the sight that immediately met her eyes. There, lying on the bed, was the blood-covered body of Thomas Huntingford. She touched his hand, which was cold. She could see that the blood on his face was congealed. It was obvious he had been dead for some time.

"What is all this?" she cried.

Sarah Huntingford replied that two men had come in and murdered Thomas, to which Mrs Jennings responded that she surely must be dreaming, or did not know what she was saying. That said, the landlady ran downstairs to fetch Samuel Beatley, then went out to call in some neighbours and a surgeon, Thomas Seeds. On returning, she went into Sarah's downstairs room, where she found the distracted woman walking to and fro and wringing her hands.

"What is all this that your husband should be so bloody?" she asked.

"He is murdered," Mrs Huntingford replied.

"How can that be when all the doors were shut?"

"Before my husband went to bed he went to the garden and I suppose he forgot to shut the door."

"Why did you not call and make a noise?" asked Mrs Jennings.

"They threatened me that if I made a noise they would murder me."

Mrs Jennings asked who the men were that threatened her.

"They were two men," she said. "One – the little one – had a lanthorn; and the tall man had something like a tomahawk. They looked black like the chimney sweepers."

Sarah said that when the men entered the room she jumped out of bed and asked them what they wanted. They answered that they wanted money but she told them they had none. At this point her husband woke up and the tall man instantly struck him on the head with the tomahawk. Thomas offered some resistance, but was killed by more blows of the tomahawk.

"I think it very odd," said Mrs Jennings, "that all this should have passed and

I should hear nothing of it, even though I sleep in the room immediately under."

"They had no shoes on and made no noise," Mrs Huntingford explained.

The surgeon, Thomas Seeds, then came down the stairs, having made a preliminary inspection of the body, and pronounced that Huntingford had died of a burst blood vessel in the lungs.

"You can't persuade me to that, for he is murdered," said the dead man's wife.

Seeds went away mumbling his protestations at the very suggestion of violence but later returned and carried out a more thorough examination. It was at this point that the wounds sustained by Mr Huntingford were discovered.

"How could you think of going into the yard and not give any alarm," asked Mrs Jennings, but Mrs Huntingford denied that she had been in the yard at all.

Other neighbours gathered in the Huntingfords' bedroom. One, a Mr Baker, observed that there was no sign of anyone other than the dead man having slept in the bed at all. Another, Mrs Ann Turnbull, pulled back the bedclothes and noted that there was indeed the impression of only one person in the bed. Later she returned to the room with Mrs Huntingford herself, and the latter went to a large open chest with little in it apart from a small wooden money box, the lid of which was forced partly off, enough to allow money to have been taken out should there have been any in there. Mrs Turnbull was then invited to examine the pockets of Huntingford's clothes which lay beside the bed. She found one pocket turned inside out, the other containing one penny and one halfpenny.

The following morning, Sunday October 25, Mrs Turnbull told Mrs Huntingford that she was under suspicion as the person who killed her husband.

"I don't care what people say or suspect as long as I am innocent," said the dead man's wife. "As everyone has condemned and is against me, I must pluck up my spirits and stand in my own defence."

Later, two constables called Carter and Wey arrived and a search was carried out. Mrs Turnbull examined the hem of Mrs Huntingford's petticoat and noticed some spots of blood on it. Mrs Huntingford rubbed it and claimed that it was not blood but dirt, or if it was blood then the garment must have lain on the bed. A further examination revealed that there was also blood smeared on one of her pockets.

"It cannot be blood," Mrs Huntingford insisted, at the same time tearing off the pocket and attempting to hide it behind the sofa. She was then arrested by the constables.

Two days later, an inquest was held. The surgeon, Seeds, spoke of a "profusion of blood" covering the bedclothes, and of discovering, on his second examination of the body, five wounds to the forehead, four of which involved fractures. There were also several other wounds, including one on the temple which was an inch in length and as wide as a half-crown and would in itself have been sufficient to cause death. The injuries appeared to have been inflicted with a heavy cutting instrument such as a billhook.

The jury had little hesitation in returning a verdict that Thomas Huntingford was murdered by his wife. But more than four months passed before trial, which excited great public interest. It lasted from 9 o'clock in the morning of Friday March 5, 1819, until 4 o'clock in the afternoon. Sarah stuck throughout to her story that her husband had been killed by two men who looked like chimney sweeps. But the jury was not convinced. Sarah was found guilty and sentenced to death.

"The evidence adduced on her trial was so irresistible," commented the *Hampshire Chronicle*, "and which she herself admitted was such as to warrant the verdict of the jury."

Sarah Huntingford kept her appointment with the executioner the following Monday, March 8, when she was drawn on a hurdle to Gallows Hill and there hanged. Her body was handed to a surgeon for dissection. She maintained her innocence to the very end.

2

THE DUELLIST IN THE DOCK
The killing of John Dieterich in 1814

The nature of the insult that prompted William Souper to challenge a fellow army officer to a duel has never been revealed. But clearly Souper thought that it left him little choice. There was a code of behaviour in such matters that officers were expected to follow. Failure to do so by either the insulted party or the person responsible for the affront could cost him not only his reputation but also his commission. Thus it was that on Wednesday April 13, 1814, Souper and John Dieterich found themselves, pistols in hand, on Pennington Common near Lymington; thus it was, two days later, that Dieterich died from the duelling injury he received; and thus it was, at the Hampshire Summer Assizes of that year, that Souper stepped into the dock to answer a charge of murder.

Duelling was an ancient custom and had for centuries been a recognized method of settling disputes of law, possession and honour. To the 20th century mind, the idea of two people trying to kill each other over a point of honour seems at best excessive and at worst barbaric, but in its heyday the duel was regarded in a very different light. In 16th century England, when its popularity was in the ascendant in the wake of similar developments in France, duelling was seen increasingly as a civilized alternative to the more savage practice of the "killing affray", in which an offended person would achieve his vengeance by arranging for his retainers, or a hired gang of assassins, to murder his enemy. The duel at least offered the prospect of a "fair fight" conducted in the presence of seconds who could ensure that it was so.

The traditional weapons of the duellist were the sword and, in the middle ages, the poleaxe, but from 1770 the pistol began to be preferred, mainly because it was likely to ensure a more even contest. In England the choice of weapon lay with the offender or challenged party, whereas in continental Europe the offended party or challenger enjoyed this right. The choice of a friend to deliver the challenge and act as second was also considered vital, especially as he could use his influence, even at the last minute, to reach a settlement without bloodshed.

These and many other customs and codes of conduct for duellists were set out in various handbooks published in the 18th and 19th centuries. One such publication advised that "the most accredited mode is to conduct the whole affair with the greatest possible politeness, expressing the challenge clearly, avoiding all strong language, simply stating, first, the cause of offence; secondly, the reason why it is considered a duty to notice the matter; thirdly, naming a friend; and lastly, requesting the appointing of a time and place".

The pervasive military atmosphere resulting from a long war with France, plus various domestic troubles, contributed to a spate of duels in the opening years of the 19th century. A large proportion involved army and navy officers, including a noteworthy encounter that occurred in Hyde Park, London, in March 1803. The protagonists were Lieutenant W of the Royal Navy and Captain I of the army and both were hit. Captain I, shot through the head, died instantly, but Lieutenant W, a ball lodged in his left breast, lived long enough to ask if his friend and adversary's wound was fatal.

"Being answered in the affirmative, he thanked Heaven he had lived thus long," says a contemporary account. "He requested a mourning ring, which was on his finger, might be given to his sister; and that she might be assured it was the happiest moment he ever knew. He had scarcely finished the word when a quantity of blood burst from his wound and he expired almost without a struggle."

Like Captain I and Lieutenant W, Captain William Henry Souper was a man of honour. Married with six children, he was an experienced soldier, with at least nineteen years service behind him, all of them during the turbulent years of the Napoleonic Wars. Army records show that as far back as September 1795, Souper was serving as a lieutenant in the 1st Battalion the 1st (or Royal) Regiment of Foot. Two years later, he transferred to the 2nd West India Regiment of Foot and in 1801 he joined the newly-formed Chasseurs Britanniques, one of a number of foreign corps raised to supplement the war effort against Napoleon's army. It was an extraordinarily cosmopolitan regiment, numbering Germans, Swiss, Italians, Poles and Croats as well as French among its officers and ranks. During its thirteen-year existence the corps saw service in various parts of the Mediterranean region and in 1807 took part in the expedition to Alexandria, when heavy casualties were suffered and a general spoke warmly of the regiment's good conduct and "unimpeachable fidelity". Later in the wars the Chasseurs Britanniques served in the Peninsula and distinguished themselves in battle at Fuentes d'Onoro and at Vitoria.

William Henry Souper served the Chasseurs Brittaniques as paymaster until 1813, the year before the corps was disbanded. At this point in his career, he was promoted to captain, apparently in the Horse Guards, and seconded to a staff appointment as paymaster at the army's Lymington depot, set up with the sole purpose of dealing with the disbandment of surplus regiments.

When Souper arrived in Lymington to take up his post at some time during the latter half of 1813 or early the following year, he found Lieutenant John Dieterich already in residence as adjutant. Dieterich was a younger and less experienced officer than Souper; he had begun his army career as an ensign in 1810 and been promoted to lieutenant eighteen months later, in March 1812. For some time he had been running the Lymington Depot without a paymaster or an assistant surgeon but now both posts were suddenly filled, the former by Captain Souper, the latter in December 1813 by John Frederick Frank.

Little is known of the relationship that developed between Souper and Dieterich during the few months in which they worked together, although the paymaster was later to refer to the adjutant as a friend whom he regarded with affection and esteem. In the middle of April 1814, however, the friendship and working relationship turned tragically sour. Souper felt Dieterich had insulted him and sought an apology, which the adjutant refused to give. Souper felt he had no option but to challenge Dieterich to a duel.

At dawn on April 13, 1814, Souper and Dieterich met near the bathing houses at Lymington, and would probably have proceeded with their affair of honour there and then but for the sudden appearance of a constable. On seeing him, they immediately got into a waiting post-chaise and drove to Woodside, and from there to Pennington Common. The constable set off in pursuit but by the time he came within sight of the common the duellists had taken up their positions and the seconds were moving back.

Left: The sword was one of the duellist's traditional weapons.

Below: Duellists using pistols were advised to stand sideways on to present the narrowest possible target.

Dieterich fired first, but missed. Captain Souper then returned fire. His shot was more accurate and Dieterich fell to the ground. The constable was now approaching, so Souper and his second returned to the chaise and drove off towards Lymington. The constable followed, but lost them before reaching the town. Returning to Pennington Common, he saw the chaise return to collect Lieutenant Dieterich, who was taken to Lymington.

"Mr Knight, a surgeon, was called in to see the Adjutant, and found a wound in the right hip which led to the backbone, from whence he extracted a ball," reported the *Hampshire Chronicle*. (Clearly Dieterich had adopted the generally recommended sideways-on stance, which presented the smallest possible target to the opponent.)

Dieterich survived for two days, but died on April 15. He was buried in Lymington churchyard and a stone was erected with an inscription, part of which read: "Sacred to the memory of John Dieterich, late Lieut. and Adjt. Of the Foreign Depot, Lymington; who unfortunately fell in a duel on the 15th day of April, 1814. In him the service has been deprived of a very meritorious officer, his wife of an excellent husband, and his children of a truly tender father."

The two seconds who had attended the duellists surrendered voluntarily, expecting to be tried for manslaughter, but the case against them was not proceeded with beyond a preliminary hearing before a grand jury. Souper, however, was arrested and held in custody at Winchester charged with the "wilful murder of John Dieterich by shooting off a pistol charged with gunpowder and a leaden bullet and giving a mortal wound on the right side, of which he languished till the 15th and then died".

An inquest jury concluded that Souper was guilty of murder and in July he found himself facing another jury at the Hampshire Assizes. Even at this stage, however, he was not pessimistic about his fate. Duellists had been tried many times in the past and the usual outcome was either an acquittal or a verdict of manslaughter and a lenient sentence. Souper had no reason to think that his case would be any different. He was not aware that the Government had recently drawn the attention of its judges to the frequency of duelling and to its determination to stamp it out.

The main facts of the case, namely that Souper and his adversary met on the "field of honour" and that the result was Dieterich's death, were not in dispute, but the defence called several gentlemen who testified as to the "general good character and humanity" of the prisoner. It was not until Mr Justice Dampier began his summing up that Souper gained the first inkling that he was in much deeper trouble than he had assumed. The judge, says a 19th century account, "laid down the law with more than usual firmness and severity". He spoke in the strongest terms of the determination of the Government to put a stop to the "fatal and too prevalent practice of duelling, as well in the Army as amongst other descriptions of persons, forced into such measures by a false sense of honour". He also warned that all persons present at or aiding and abetting a duel were, in the eye of the law, principals and subject to capital punishment.

"We hope and trust," commented the *Hampshire Chronicle* in its report of the trial, "that the impressive manner in which this was intimated by the Learned Judge will have its due effect and prevent a practice disgraceful to a civilized society and pregnant with such consequences, as this unfortunate and unhappy prisoner feels he has brought on himself and family."

Souper is said to have listened to the judge's summing up with growing anxiety. "He was," says one report, "a married man with a family of children; he had watched the earlier proceedings with some indifference; he knew the Grand Jury had thrown out the bill against the seconds, and in his own case he expected the common result, either a verdict of acquittal or at most manslaughter, followed by a short imprisonment. But the tone of the judge's summing up roused him from his dream; he fully understood the import of every word that fell from the bench, and he listened with increasing alarm. Sometimes there was even a slight movement in his face, as of spasm; but in all other respects he maintained his perfect composure."

The jury spent thirty minutes considering their verdict and the delay went some way towards reviving the waning hopes of Souper and his defenders. But their optimism was short-lived. Amid an atmosphere of acute tension and breathless silence, the jury announced its verdict: "Guilty of murder." The shock was too much for Souper. Hardly had the foreman uttered the three words than the prisoner "fell down as if shot with a mortal wound, and amid the profoundest silence of the audience, uttered one long, loud groan". Several minutes passed before he recovered sufficiently to enable the proceedings to be resumed.

Asked if he had anything to say why sentence of death should not be passed on him according to law, Souper began by apologizing for the interruption he had given to the business of the court, which he said he hoped would not be imputed to the fear of death, which he had faced unmoved in the field of battle, and the more fatal climate of the West Indies. But he had a wife and children to whom he had trusted to bequeath his only fortune – the unstained character of a soldier and a man of honour.

"But now," he told the court, "I am to die the death of a felon, to leave my six children the infamy of a murderer. They now can only behold me with abhorrence."

Souper said he had spent a long life in the service of his country, he hoped with honour and credit. He had also intended his sons for the same profession. But now his hopes were blasted; life rendered insupportable; his future destiny indifferent.

Turning to the circumstances of the duel that had brought him to this position, he stressed that it was his adversary who was the aggressor, who had publicly offered him an insult he dared not overlook. He had been willing to accept any apology, he said; but none was forthcoming. This left him with no alternative but to send a challenge or lose his commission; for if he had not sent a challenge to vindicate his honour, and the honour of the service, the next post would have brought an intimation from the Horse Guards that the king had no further occasion for his services. Souper also drew the court's attention to the paradox that a practice authorised and encouraged by the British army at the highest level should attract the severest penalty of the British law.

Speaking of Lieutenant John Dieterich, Souper said he remembered him with affection and regret. He bitterly lamented that a false idea of honour had precluded a friend whom he esteemed from yielding an apology that would have prevented the result he now deplored.

"And for this," he concluded, "I am to be led to execution like the vilest felon and murderer."

Souper's address was long and impressive, and it was delivered in a "firm voice and a manly style of speaking". It had a profound effect on everyone in the courtroom. "Scarcely a dry eye was seen, and in many parts of the crowded court loud sobs proclaimed the due sympathy excited," reported the Hampshire Chronicle. "The judge was taken by surprise; he was an able and good man, and full of the kindest feelings. He listened attentively, and was obviously much interested. Soon he stooped forward, and, leaning on his elbows, rested his chin upon one hand clenched; presently, he added the other, clenching both hands, apparently to control his emotions. At length, tears started from his eyes and rolled down his fine manly face; he raised his head, unclenched his hands, and covered his face, still leaning on his elbows, and then awaited the end of Captain Souper's appeal."

Nevertheless, given the verdict, there was only one course immediately open to Mr Justice Dampier and that was to sentence Souper to death by hanging.

The execution was fixed for Monday July 25 and it was also ordered that Souper's body be delivered to Mr Giles King Lyford, a surgeon, to be "dissected and anatomized pursuant to the statute in that behalf".

Dampier, however, made the strongest representations on behalf of the condemned officer. The government was not easily persuaded, such was its newfound determination on the matter of duelling, but Dampier was insistent, and since it was not then the custom to execute against the wishes of the presiding judge, Souper was eventually pardoned.

What happened to him after that has not hitherto been known, but an examination of army records reveals that he resumed his military career within a very short time. The Lymington depot had been abolished by the end of 1814 but by the spring of 1815, Souper was serving as paymaster at the army depot at Harwich, along with surgeon John Frederick Frank, who had served with him and Dieterich at the Lymington depot. Interestingly, the adjutant's job at Harwich is shown as vacant and appears to have remained so throughout Souper's stay there.

It is also clear that, following his pardon, Souper was able to reinstate his plan for at least one of his sons to join the services. In May 1815, William Henry Souper junior was commissioned as ensign in the York Chasseurs. He was promoted to lieutenant in 1817 and remained a serving officer until his premature death in 1820.

The career of Souper senior, meanwhile, went on and on. From 1819 onwards, he appears in the Army List as a recruiting district paymaster on half-pay, which he remained until 1835, when he retired after a career spanning at least forty years.

As Captain William Henry Souper neared the end of his life, duelling was also nearing the end of its own existence in an increasingly disapproving Britain. As the spirit of the 19th century took hold, as the aristocratic gave way to the bourgeois, and the military to the civilian, the duel gradually became less fashionable. From the period of Souper's duel onwards, the duellist risked not only death at the hands of his adversary but condemnation from the public and conviction and sentence for murder in the courts. Some duels did still take place, of course, especially in the army and the higher echelons (the Duke of Wellington, while he was prime minister, in 1829, called out Lord Winchilsea and took a shot at him and the Earl of Cardigan wounded a Captain Tuckett in a duel in 1840 – he was tried by the House of Lords, but acquitted), but by the middle of the century duelling was a matter of history in the British Isles.

3
THE SON OF SATAN
The murder of Mary Hall in 1862

One night in the middle of June 1862, farmer's daughter Mary Hall awoke with a start. She had been woken by a bad dream and was relieved to find herself safe and well in her own bed. Even so, she found the nature of the dream disturbing.

"I dreamt," she said at breakfast the following morning, "that I was going to be put to death by someone who would not give me time to say my prayers, even though I earnestly begged for time to do so."

Her family reacted as most people would react. They listened interestedly, smiled reassuringly, then passed off the subject as a joke. But it was not a joke. In fact, the dream was frighteningly prophetic. Within four days, it was to turn into a waking nightmare as Mary was attacked and brutally murdered on her way to church.

Mary Ann Susan Hall was twenty-three years old and a model of God-fearing respectability. As the *Hampshire Chronicle* put it, she had for a long time "been in the habit of attending church twice on Sundays, and she bore a high moral character in the neighbourhood". Her mother had been dead some years and she lived with her father, William Hall, and her stepmother at Midgham Farm, a mile to the southwest of Fordingbridge, not far from the Hampshire-Dorset border. She was an attractive young woman, and a popular one in the local community, and was engaged to marry one of her cousins. She was her father's only child and he doted on her.

It was Mary Hall's practice to walk to and from church every Sunday morning and again in the evening. Her route took her along a lonely footpath overlooked by a wooded hillside sloping steeply down from the ridge on which the farmhouse stood to the marshy lowland and the gently flowing River Avon below. Mary thought nothing of the journey, having walked it so many times before, but for some the area had a fearful reputation for tragedy and dastardly deeds. Here, two or three years earlier, two cows had been found with their tongues cut out. Here, a man called Joseph West had been killed when he fell out of a tree. And here George Hanning had died when a cart pulled by a runaway horse toppled over and crushed him.

On the morning of Sunday June 22, 1862, Mary set off for church for what was to be the last time. She was dressed in her best white bonnet, decorated with green flowers, a mantel or cloak with silk tassels at the back, and kid gloves. She carried a parasol and, as was her custom on Sundays, two books – a church service book and a hymn book. She left Midgham Farm at 10 o'clock, watched by her father's live-in dairymaid, Helen Smith, who saw her take the footpath and set off in the direction of Fordingbridge.

Mary was expected home for dinner at 1 o'clock but she did not arrive. "I expect she've gone to Court Farm with her cousins," speculated her step-mother.

Nothing was heard of Mary until 4 o'clock, when a labourer called George Gilbert went to see the local policeman to report the discovery of a woman's body. He was carrying a parasol that, he told the constable, he had found on the ground while walking across a field called Harding's Field. He had found the woman farther on, in Holmes Lane, a sunken track or ditch with water up to two feet deep in places, that formed the boundary between Harding's Field and William Hall's farm.

The constable rounded up a small party of people, including a surgeon, and Gilbert led them to the spot. The woman was obviously dead. She lay with her arms outstretched and fists clenched, her clothes "fearfully torn and thickly covered with mud and slime of the ditch, through which evidently she had been dragged". On her breast was her church service book and in one hand she still clutched her hymn book. Some members of the party recognized her as Mary Hall and, helped by George Gilbert, they carried her to her father's house, one window of which was within sight – though not within earshot – of the place where she had been killed.

Above: Midgham Farmhouse today.
(Photo: Bob Richardson)

Right: Murder Stile, near Fordingbridge,
today. *(Photo: Bob Richardson)*

It was immediately obvious that Mary had been the victim of an attempted sexual assault; her underclothes were in tatters. It was also clear that she had made a brave attempt to ward off her attacker. There was evidence of a struggle at a stile sited at the boundary of Farmer Hall's land and Harding's, and it seemed that her attacker, having gained the upper hand, had dragged her fifteen yards along the ditch, which was screened from the view of any passers-by by furze bushes on either side.

"Here it was," reported the *Hampshire Chronicle*, "that the second struggle took place, the girl having been evidently placed against the side of the ditch, with the lower part of her body trailing in the mud, while the brute attempted to carry out his infernal purpose. From this spot, then, he dragged his victim by the legs for the distance of 140 yards through the water, filth, and weeds of the ditch, screened from all human observation by the overhanging bushes, finally putting the now lifeless body in the place and position in which it was found."

It also appeared that Mary was still alive when her head was immersed in the stinking ditch water. Her mouth, nose and ears were full of mud and some had also reached her stomach.

"I am of opinion that death resulted from violence, partly from strangulation, and partly from immersion," reported Thomas Rake, the Quaker surgeon who carried out the post mortem examination. "I do not think that the body was dead when first immersed. If it had been there would have been more water in the lungs and less in the stomach."

As to whether she had been raped, Mr Rake, at this stage, was uncertain.

"The ordinary marks of violation were absent, but the evidence on this point is entirely negative. There might or might not have been an attempt," he said.

Within hours of Mary Hall's body being discovered, a man was under arrest and facing a charge of murder. He was 30-year-old George Jacob Gilbert, the man who had reported the tragic discovery to the police and who had helped to carry the limp corpse to the farmhouse.

George Gilbert, alias George Philpott, was well known to the Hall family, having worked for Mary's father as a farm labourer in the past. He was particularly well known to Mary, who had been trying to rid herself of his unwanted attentions for some time. She had told her family and friends of her fear of him and on at least two previous occasions she had met him on the same footpath.

"On these occasions," reported the *Chronicle*, "she was in company, and the only molestation she received from him was his offering his hand to help her over the stile, which she refused."

Gilbert, for his part, made no secret of his interest in the attractive young daughter of his former employer. Four or five weeks before the tragedy, he was with his friend John Turner when Mary Hall walked past them on her way to church. She chose to leave the footpath briefly to pass them before rejoining it a little further on.

"Anybody might go and have all she got, and nobody know anything about it," Gilbert said as the young woman continued her journey. After a pause, he added: "There she goes."

A fortnight later, again on a Sunday morning, Gilbert called at Turner's house and invited him to come for a walk. After a tour of the allotment gardens at Fordingbridge, Gilbert suggested going to Midgham Moor.

"We went, and got there just as the bells struck out for church," Turner recalled later. "As we were going through Mr Thompson's field, called Lapersey, we met Miss Hall. She was coming towards Fordingbridge Church. We sat on Mr Thompson's stile in the same field. Miss Hall passed us before that. Gilbert said he should like to have connection with her, and added: 'Miss Hall is a nice young girl, isn't she?' That was after she had passed, and when I asked why her particularly more than other girls, he said there was perhaps not much difference between her and other girls, but there was a little more fancy."

On the eve of Mary's death, Gilbert asked Turner if he would go for a walk with him the next morning. Asked where, Gilbert simply replied: "Somewhere for a stroll."

"I asked him where he called somewhere," Turner recalled, "and he replied, 'Somewhere for a walk, the same as usual.' From what he said, I thought he meant to abuse Miss Hall."

George Gilbert was a tragic figure. An illegitimate child, he had been born into a 19th century England that did not suffer the unfortunate gladly. He was from the start deprived of security, opportunity, and parental control and guidance. He never knew his mother and, in the view of the *Hampshire Chronicle*, had a father whom it would have been better for him not to know. Left to himself, he associated with "idle" boys and, as he grew into manhood, joined a gang of poachers. "The influence of this class of persons upon his character was just what might be expected, and drove him from one act of outlawry to another," the *Chronicle* observed.

By 1862, he had a long criminal record which included convictions for rape, burglary, highway robbery and a string of lesser offences. For one burglary, he had been condemned to seven years transportation, although he appears to have served his sentence in this country, first at Portland Prison in Dorset, where he suffered an accident that adversely affected his health, and then on the convict hulk Stirling Castle at Portsmouth. Released, he assaulted and robbed a young woman on the highway, for which he was sentenced to four years penal servitude, all of which he served in Gibraltar. His most recent spell in prison had been in February 1862, when he served a short custodial sentence for poaching.

On the evening of June 22, after being arrested and charged with murder, Gilbert told Constable Rodaway, the arresting officer: "I've been in pretty near such a mess as this before and I don't care so long as they don't hang me."

Gilbert was interviewed by Superintendent Stannard, who came up from Ringwood to lead the murder investigation. Stannard also examined Gilbert's clothes and found that his trousers were wet up to a point above the knees and that there was stinking mud inside the legs near the bottom. Stockings and the sleeves of a shirt, recovered from the house in Frog Lane, Fordingbridge, where Gilbert lived with his half-brother and sister-in-law, Charles and Caroline Philpott, were also wet and muddy, though the prisoner denied they were his.

The continuing police inquiries produced a number of witnesses who had seen Gilbert in the Midgham Moor area on the day in question. One was Helen Smith, William Hall's dairymaid, who, a few hours after seeing her master's daughter set off for church, left to make the same journey herself.

"I left the farm to go to a christening in the afternoon," she said. "I met Gilbert in the lane, between John Gilbert's and Attman's new house, not a great distance from the church. He was smoking and he had his working clothes on. It was about a quarter before three. He was coming towards Holmes' Lane, where the body was found, about a quarter-of-a-mile distant. He did not speak to me nor I to him."

The information offered by labourer Robert Haskell, of Mudsmore, was even more incriminating.

"On the Sunday morning," he said, "I had occasion to go to Harbridge to see my daughter. I went along the footpath leading to Midgham about half-past ten. Where the body was found the dew was beaten off the grass, as if there had been a 'scamper' there. I saw that something had passed or been dragged up the water. Thorns, nettles, brambles and all sorts of bushes are growing in the hedge. I saw a treading of feet from the stile up to the water. Afterwards, on looking towards Bickton, I saw the prisoner coming up under the hedge. I watched him. He wore a brown smock frock, and was wet up to his knees. He had his boots on but they were unlaced. I did not speak to him. I saw the cows in an uproar, which made me look over the hedge. They were in the same field as the prisoner. When I left, the prisoner was leaning against an ash tree."

At 11.15, Gilbert was seen again, this time by shepherd John Gosney. He said Gilbert was standing in the ditch, leaning against the bank, picking something off his clothes. "When he saw me, he got out of the ditch and walked off quite smart so that I could not speak to him," added Gosney.

The following day, an inquest was opened at the victim's home for the purpose of identification and was later continued at the Greyhound Inn, Fordingbridge, with Gilbert present. He betrayed no emotion and told the coroner: "All I have to say is that I know nothing about it, except that I found the body lying in the lane."

When the three-stage inquest was again resumed at the Greyhound on Tuesday June 24, the jury unanimously returned a verdict of wilful murder against Gilbert. After the hearing, the prisoner asked Constable Rodaway if he thought it was "a hanging touch". The officer said he did not know but that the very thought of it made him ill.

"So it do me," said Gilbert. "I don't feel right and shall be glad to get rid of it. This is the last time I shall be brought here."

Mary Hall was buried beside the remains of her grandfather at the family plot at Breamore, four miles from Midgham Farm. It was a desperately sad occasion, as the *Hampshire Chronicle* reporter described.

"The funeral cortege left the house at one o'clock," he wrote, "and wended its way to Fordingbridge, where a large number of tradesmen joined, and followed in vehicles, forming one of the most melancholy processions it has been our lot to witness. The whole of the shops in the route were closed, and the blinds of the private houses were drawn. At Breamore the mournful pageant was augmented, the whole consisting of thirteen vehicles. On arriving at the church, the corpse (being borne by six cousins of the deceased) was met by the Rev J. N. Palmer, the curate, who read the service in a most impressive manner. At the grave, the deep emotion of the Reverend gentleman was apparent to all present – he could scarcely proceed with the ceremony – and not a dry eye was to be observed amongst those assembled. It was indeed a most affecting scene."

Eight days after Mary Hall's death, Gilbert was brought up on remand at Fordingbridge police station before one of the county magistrates, Mr J Coventry. The venue was chosen in preference to the usual court at Ringwood in the interests of public order and the prisoner's own safety. The police had already had difficulty in protecting him from a lynch-mob that had gathered at Ringwood railway station for his last departure by train to Winchester Prison.

"The affair has created great excitement in the neighbourhood and the scene of the murder has been visited by thousands of persons," said the *Hampshire Chronicle* in its report of the Fordingbridge hearing. "Owing to the excited state of the people, it was thought desirable that the prisoner, who since his first examination had been confined in Winchester Jail, should be taken as privately as possible to Fordingbridge. He was consequently removed thither during divine service Sunday afternoon, to be in readiness for his examination next day."

Publicly, Gilbert appeared calm. He displayed much bravado, even answering back as the mob shouted threats and threatened to engulf him at Ringwood station. But in court he looked pale and dejected, and it was said that his true state of mind was very low. A rope and noose made from his bedclothes had been found in his cell, suggesting that he had already contemplated suicide.

Helen Smith, Robert Haskell, John Gosney and James Turner were among those who gave evidence at the preliminary hearing at Fordingbridge. So was Caroline Philpott, wife of Gilbert's half-brother. She said Gilbert took breakfast with them on the day in question and went out around 9.30, not returning, as far as she was aware, before dinner time. In the afternoon, she went for a walk with her little girl and met Gilbert with a parasol in his hand.

"Where on earth has't found that?" she asked him, to which he replied that he had found it "down in Harding's flying about, and the cows making a great noise". He then told her he had seen a woman in a ditch, covered in mud, and she advised him to tell the police.

Gilbert's trial began at the Summer Assizes in Winchester on Friday July 19, 1862, amid an atmosphere of immense public excitement. People looked upon Gilbert more as a monster than a man and they were calling him "the Son of Satan". Within minutes of the doors being opened, the courtroom was packed to overflowing, every nook and cranny occupied, and hundreds still outside unable to gain admission.

The prisoner, described as a "slightly-made man, thin but muscular, pale countenance, and rather intelligent-looking, and not at all so ill-favoured as represented in several published reports of his examination before the magistrates", behaved quietly and calmly in the dock, entered his plea of Not Guilty in a respectful tone and manner and chose not to challenge any of the twelve jurymen.

Opening the case for the prosecution, Mr Prideaux described how, as early as 10.30 on June 22, a piece of green ornament and a tassel had been found, by a witness named Nicklen, between two stiles at the point where the footpath from Midgham Farm to Fordingbridge church joined Holmes Lane. The cows in the adjoining field were in a very excited state and there was clear evidence of a struggle. Later, at the end of Holmes Lane, was found the body of the deceased, her throat and mouth filled with mud, marks of violence on her throat, her dress disordered, wet and torn and covered in mud.

"The evidence will prove beyond doubt that the murder was effected after much violence," said Mr Prideaux. "The deceased evidently struggled hard in resisting the attack upon her; and by the sacrificing of her life, she only preserved her honour. It is a matter of rejoicing that there is this one gleam of light in the melancholy case. The evidence of the surgeon is such as to afford some comfort to the jury and the sorrowing friends and family of the deceased, for it is clear that although the unfortunate girl struggled to the death to resist the attempt, she struggled successfully, and passed through nature to eternity pure as she had been during her innocent life."

Twenty-two prosecution witnesses were called, many of whom had already told their stories at the inquest and the preliminary magisterial hearing. The Assize Court also heard from Charles and Caroline Philpott's young son, who told how, later on the Sunday, he saw Uncle George hanging his stockings on the line, and how he also remarked that his uncle's trousers were very wet. Another witness was the sexton of St Mary's Church, Fordingbridge, a man called Jefferies, who was working with Gilbert, and drinking cider with him, on the evening before the murder, when he particularly noticed that his companion's boots were nailed all around the bottoms and not just on the heels and toes. On going to the scene of the murder the following day, he saw footprints corresponding with these boots, but they were soon obliterated by the assembled crowd.

The prosecution also presented the victim's clothing to the court as exhibits, and the pathetic garments presented a "shocking spectacle". Mary's bonnet was "completely crushed and crumpled up into a dirty rag", while her dress, underclothes and mantel were in a "fearful mess".

The array of evidence produced against the prisoner at the bar was formidable, though circumstantial. The defending counsel, Mr Bere, called not a single witness and his client did not go into the witness box.

"I stand in a most awful and responsible position," said Mr Bere, launching into an emotive speech directed as much towards the hearts of the jury as to their minds and the facts of the case. "Ere the prisoner's life or death being decided on, there is only to come my speech, the judge's summing-up and the verdict of the jury, and as what I say might influence the prisoner's fate, I feel my position is a terrible one. The accused has but one representative, whilst against him is a case instituted and supported by the public purse – the best of all to go to – and the highest skill and experience of the bar to sustain it. All the public sympathy is for the deceased and against the prisoner, the only man charged with having brought about her death."

Urging the jury to put aside all prejudicial and sympathetic feelings, he added: "Public indignation, led by the public press, has condemned the prisoner by a foregone conclusion of his guilt, and there is no refuge remaining for the accused but a wise and impartial judge and an honest English jury."

Mr Bere claimed that there appeared to be a "determination on the part of the witnesses for the prosecution to do their best against the prisoner". "Most of them are natives of the parish where the murder took place," he said, "and for the credit, as it were, of the place, they are anxious that the offender shall not escape punishment, and no doubt they honestly believe that the prisoner at the bar is the offender."

Stressing the circumstantial nature of the evidence, Mr Bere said that if nearness to the body were to be taken as evidence, then the case against the prosecution witness Robert Haskell was stronger than that against Gilbert. And as to Gilbert's boots and clothes being wet and muddy, there were numerous places over the adjacent moors where he could have got into such a state.

"The case for the prisoner is explainable," he went on. "He sees the cows excited and looking into the hedge; he runs down and finds the body in the ditch. His conduct is consistent with his innocence. If guilty, could he be so mad as to go and give information even to the officers of the law, by whom he must have known a hue and cry would be raised immediately to find the criminal?"

Mr Bere concluded by delivering an "impressive allusion" to the horrors of capital punishment, urging the jury to hesitate before submitting the prisoner to such a fate in the absence of conclusive evidence of his guilt.

His appeal was in vain. It took the jury a mere fifteen minutes to conclude that Gilbert was the murderer of Mary Hall.

"The quiet of the court at the decisive moment was so great that the answers of the foreman of the jury were distinctly heard at the doors of the hall, and when the nature of the verdict was heard by the large crowd of people outside, there was immediately a loud clapping of hands," reported the *Chronicle*. "The judge directed that some officers should be sent out to suppress the noise, and any person who was guilty of the indecent conduct should be taken into custody. The prisoner made no reply when asked if he had anything to say in arrest of judgement."

The judge put on the black cap amidst breathless silence, at which moment observers noticed a slight flushing of Gilbert's cheeks. This was, however, the only sign of emotion from him; throughout the trial his features had remained "indifferent, unchanged and unaltered to all outward appearance". The judge, on the other hand, was clearly much affected by his onerous duty and was almost in tears as he told Gilbert that his crime was one committed "under circumstances of so aggravated a nature that they prevent almost the possibility of the case finding a parallel in the history of crime". Passing sentence of death, he added: "Time will be given to you – that time and opportunity which you denied to your unhappy victim – for you hurried her to her great account wholly unprepared to meet it. The law shall be more merciful to you; you shall have some time at least to think over your past career in this world and to prepare for that which is to come."

Gilbert's execution was fixed for Monday August 4, by which time the unbroken reserve he had shown, at least publicly, throughout his period on remand and during the trial, had finally broken and he had made a full confession to the murder. More than that, the prison chaplain was unwilling to reveal.

The execution was to be carried out publicly over the gateway to the county prison by William Calcraft, a former ladies' shoemaker, now one of the better-known members of his rather exclusive profession. During his forty-six years as executioner, he had built a reputation for being a kindly, mild-mannered man but also one whose method of hanging was "very rough, much the same as if he had been hanging a dog". He was a "short-drop man" whose methods resulted in a high proportion of failures and it was not uncommon for him to go below the gallows "just to steady their legs a little" – in other words, to add his own weight to that of the hanging body!

Such was the strength of public feeling against George Gilbert that his appointment with Calcraft attracted an even greater crowd than usual to the gates of the county prison. The crowds began to assemble at an early hour and a few people even took up their positions the previous evening. Soon the crowd numbered around 10,000 and it included a large number of women. The majority came on foot, but some were in gigs and others on horseback, and many brought their opera glasses to obtain a better view of the proceedings. Their behaviour was unexpectedly orderly.

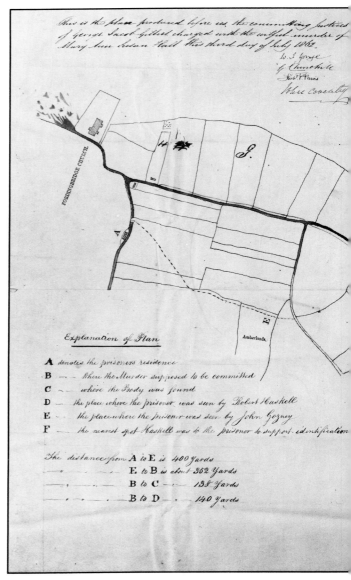

A map produced at George Gilbert's trial showing Fordingbridge Church (top left) and Midgham Farm (bottom right). Gilbert's home is indicated by the letter A; the scene of the murder by the letter B.

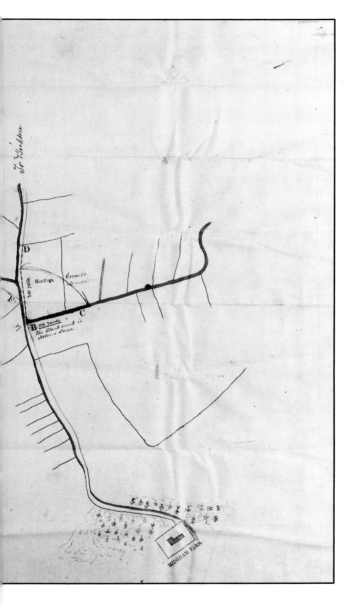

"The multitude could not be called a mob," the *Hampshire Chronicle* tells us, "but a mass or crowd of people, most of whom were respectably dressed. We know on undoubted authority that the feeling against the prisoner was strong and it was expected that it would have been very unequivocally expressed by the people. Indeed, we know the prison officials were quite expecting some outburst of feeling when the procession appeared over the gateway. We know also that some of the crowd were saying before Gilbert was seen that they would not mind hanging him themselves; but as soon as the unfortunate man stood upon the drop, the same persons ejaculated 'poor fellow'."

Gilbert himself was attended early by the chaplain, who stayed with him until the clock struck eight and the sheriff's officers arrived to collect him. The prisoner then walked with a firm step to the pinioning room, which adjoined the top of the gateway, site of the execution. The chaplain led the procession, as at a funeral, but before they emerged from the prison building into the courtyard, he moved back and walked alongside Gilbert talking with him as they went.

In the pinioning room, Calcraft passed a broad strap of strong leather around the prisoner's waist and bound his arms above the elbows with short buckled straps.

"While this was being done, and even on the way to the room, the man audibly uttered words which seemed to be prayers for mercy on his soul," wrote the *Chronicle's* reporter at the event. "That portion of the funeral service usually read on such occasions then commenced, and was continued until the drop fell. Life was soon extinct, but there was an unusual continuance of muscular convulsions, the criminal being possessed of extraordinary vital power."

The report continued: "The only sympathetic exhibition of feeling on the part of the crowd was when the drop fell, but it ceased before the man was dead, and the vast multitude stood eagerly watching the convulsive struggles of the dying man. There was no groaning by the populace, as has been stated in some papers. Women seemed to endure the sight more firmly even than men. One man actually fainted as the drop fell, and was carried away from the sight. There were some two or three persons, including the Secretary of the Open Air Mission, preaching amongst the crowd, and several others were distributing tracts. Three thousand religious tracts were distributed in a few minutes by two or three persons, who said they were nothing amongst the multitude. After the body had hung the usual time, it was taken down and, we believe, a cast of the head was taken and the body then interred according to the sentence of the judge 'within the precincts of the prison'."

The people of Fordingbridge never forgave the man who deprived them of the much-loved young woman from Midgham Farm; nor did they forget him. One hundred and forty years after the tragedy, the locals still talk of the killer their ancestors called Satan's Son. And they still refer to the spot where Mary Hall died as Murder Stile.

There was one person whom fate gave little opportunity to forgive George Gilbert. Childless and grief-stricken, Mary's father lost his will to live and followed her to the grave within a short time of his daughter's death.

Several months later, a man called Parker was working at Charles and Caroline Philpott's Frog Lane cottage when he stumbled across one additional piece of evidence linking Gilbert with the murdered girl. Parker was removing a portion of the thatched roof of the house where Gilbert had lived when he discovered, hidden in the thatch, trinkets that Mary Hall had worn on the day of her death.

4

HORROR IN THE HOP GARDEN

The murder of Fanny Adams in 1867

On a warm Saturday evening during the summer of 1867, a solicitors clerk and former Sunday school teacher penned an extraordinary entry in the diary he kept among the legal papers at his office in the Hampshire town of Alton. It was an entry as cold and emotionless as it was brief. It began with the date – Saturday August 24 – and added simply: "Killed a young girl. It was fine and hot."

A few hours earlier, eight-year-old Fanny Adams had left her home in Tanhouse Lane, near Alton church, for the last time. It was about 1.30 p.m. when she went out to play with her younger sister, Lizzie, and her friend, Minnie Warner, also aged eight, and they headed for a spot called Flood Meadow, 400 yards from home. Soon they noticed a man sitting on a gate, a stranger dressed in a black frock coat, light waistcoat and trousers and a tall black hat. The man beckoned to Fanny, calling her towards him. All three girls approached and he played with them for a short time and picked some berries for them to eat. He also offered them some money, giving three halfpence to Lizzie and Minnie with the suggestion that they go and buy some sweets, and offering Fanny a halfpenny to accompany him to the Hollow, an old road leading to the village of Shalden. Fanny took the money but refused to go with him, upon which the man picked her up and carried her into a nearby hop-field. As Minnie and Lizzie set off, they heard Fanny start to cry and the man tell her: "Don't cry, my dear. Keep quiet, and if you come with me into the hop garden, I'll give you some more money."

It was the last time Fanny Adams was seen alive. At 5 p.m., when the youngster failed to come home for tea, her mother Harriet Adams began a search with neighbour Jane Gardener and young Minnie Warner. They failed to find Fanny but saw a man coming out of a field.

"That's the man who gave us the pennies," Minnie blurted out.

The man corrected her: "No, it was three halfpennies I gave you, and the others a halfpenny."

Mrs Gardener took hold of the man and demanded to know his name.

"No matter what's my name. You'll find me at Mr Clement's office if you want me," he replied.

Mrs Gardener asked him where the missing child was, but he claimed he had not seen her since he left the girls playing at the gate. The man spoke quietly and gave an impression of respectability. Mrs Gardener apologized if she had mistaken him for an "old gentleman who has been giving halfpennies to the children for no good purpose" and the two women went home confident that Fanny was playing on her own in the fields somewhere and would return before long. Their optimism was unjustified. The church clock struck seven, there was still no sign of young Fanny and between then and 8 o'clock, a search party was organized by the neighbours.

A labourer called James Gates made the first discovery. He was searching in a hop garden belonging to a Mr Chalcraft when he saw, first, a blood-stained piece of clothing and then the severed head of a young girl. The head, which was on the ground between two hop poles, was covered in dirt and the eyes were missing, having apparently been gouged out. (They were later found in the River Wey nearby.) Twenty yards from the scene of his first discovery, Gates found a child's leg and, further on, the torso, which he described as having been "cut open like a sheep which had been killed".

With a lack of sensitivity that defies belief, Gates carried the severed head to the Adams family's cottage where, in the words of a contemporary newspaper, "all doubts were then set at rest, the poor mother identifying the head as that of her daughter, and immediately falling into hysterics". Harriet Adams rushed off to find her husband, who was playing cricket some distance away, but collapsed before reaching him and had to be taken home. When George Adams did get a message telling him of the tragedy, he hastened home, seized a loaded gun, and went out to kill the man who had given the children money and, surely, had murdered Fanny. He failed to find him.

In the meantime, more discoveries were being made in and around the hop garden. As the *Hampshire Chronicle* reported on August 31, a "sickening spectacle" had the effect of "completely paralysing for a time" those engaged in the search. Little Fanny's body had been hacked to pieces and the many parts scattered around. Most of them, including her heart, were found in the hop garden but her left foot and left arm were in a field nearby, where they had apparently been thrown with sufficient force to carry them over two high hedges and a lane. The lungs and intestines and one arm were not found until the following morning.

One contemporary account records: "The body displayed several fearful stabs and gashes, the ribs being severely punctured, the calves of the legs and thighs had been completely ripped up, and the intestines entirely removed, leaving the mere frame of the body only. The right ear was picked up in a corner of the hop-field by itself. No traces of the eyes were at this time discovered, and the right breast was also missing. In consequence of the disjointed and mutilated condition of the whole body, it is impossible for the medical gentlemen who have examined the remains to determine whether the poor child had been violated."

The girl's remains were taken in a trunk to Alton police station, where they were examined by a police surgeon, Dr Louis Leslie. He concluded that dismemberment had been carried out after death. He also found, on the severed head, a wound probably inflicted by a blow from a stone so severe that the scalp had been completely divided.

Police officers involved in the early stages of the investigation were soon able to obtain a description of the man with whom Fanny Adams had last been seen. Helped by his local knowledge, Superintendent Cheyney concluded that the description matched that of a man named Frederick Baker, who worked for Clement's, a firm of solicitors in Alton. Cheyney arrived there between 8 and 9 o'clock that evening and found 29-year-old Baker sitting at his desk, working. He asked Baker if he had heard about the murder.

"Yes," Baker replied. "And they say it's me, don't they?"

Told that he was indeed under suspicion, Baker responded: "I am innocent and willing to go where you like."

Cheyney asked if Baker had any knives on him, at which he produced two – one with a buckhorn handle and another with a white handle that had a small smear of blood on it. Later that evening, still protesting his innocence, Baker was taken into custody. A large crowd had already gathered outside the police station

THE ILLUSTRATED
POLICE NEWS.
LAW-COURTS AND WEEKLY RECORD

No. 187.]   LONDON, SATURDAY, SEPTEMBER 14, 1867.   [PRICE ONE PENNY

THE ALTON MURDER.
PORTRAIT OF FANNY ADAMS.

HOUSE IN WHICH THE PARENTS OF THE MURDERED CHILD RESIDE.

THE HOUSE LANE AND FIELD, WHERE THE MURDERER MET HIS VICTIM.

A MAN ATTACKED BY AN ELEPHANT.

ATTEMPTED SCHOLARY AT GREENWICH.—COURAGEOUS SERVANT.

HOUSE IN MILSTEAD TERRACE

PORTRAIT OF THE PRISONERS.

THE MURDER OF EMMA SNOW.

THE TRAGEDY IN THE OLD KENT ROAD.

MELANCHOLY ACCIDENT IN A HARVEST FIELD AT ROMFORD.

The Alton murder makes the front page of the *Illustrated Police News*.

and their mood and behaviour was such that the prisoner had to be smuggled through a back entrance for his own safety. Once in the cell, he was searched and stripped and his clothes examined. His light tweed trousers were found to be marked with blood and both legs were still damp, apparently from recent washing. Baker's socks were also wet, the front of his waistcoat bore splashes of blood and the wristbands of his shirt were soaked with blood. Even his boots were wet and officers suspected that he had washed them in a stream near the spot where Fanny Adams was killed. Asked to account for the state of his clothing, Baker said that he could not except to say that he was in the habit, when out, of stepping into water, hence his wet trouserlegs.

On the Tuesday following Fanny's death, the Hampshire deputy coroner, Robert Harfield, opened an inquest at the Duke's Head Inn, Alton. Frederick Baker was among those present, looking, according to the *Hampshire Chronicle*, "pale but self-possessed". Little Minnie Warner was the first to give evidence but – frightened as she was by the large crowd, staring in through the pub windows and chattering excitedly – she was unable to pick out Baker as the man who took Fanny away. Fanny's parents also had to take the stand, George Adams being almost overcome by grief as he talked of identifying his daughter's remains the previous weekend.

One witness, Ann Murrant, told the inquest that she saw Baker twice on the Saturday afternoon. On the first occasion, at about 3 o'clock, he was walking along the footpath towards Alton and was wearing a pair of light trousers and a high hat. Between 5 and 6 o'clock she saw him again near the church. As he crossed the churchyard and went towards the Hollow, he stared hard at her and her little girl, which made her notice him particularly. As he went up the path, he kept looking round at them.

Another clerk at the solicitor's office, Maurice Biddle, said he saw Baker in the office at about 6 o'clock on the Saturday and Baker told him about his conversation with a woman about a missing child, adding that it would be very awkward for him if the child were found murdered. The two men had then adjourned to the Swan tap for a glass of ale, where Baker announced that he was going away the following Monday. He said he planned to go with the hotel boot-cleaner.

"The 'boots' said he could turn his hand to anything but Baker could not; and Baker replied, 'Yes, I could turn butcher'," Biddle told the inquest.

He added that he saw Baker again in the office later that evening and told him that people were saying that he murdered the child, to which his colleague replied: "Never, Maurice. It's a bad job for me, then."

Questioned by a juror, Biddle said Baker had told him that he had drunk gin and beer on the Saturday morning.

"He was sometimes under the influence of liquor," Biddle added.

The police offered in evidence the diary found in Baker's desk drawer with its entry – "Killed a young girl" – for the day of the murder. Superintendent Cheyney said Baker had admitted that the entry was in his handwriting.

Asked by the deputy coroner if he had anything to say, Baker replied: "No, Sir, only that I am innocent."

In his summary, the deputy coroner told the jury that there was no direct evidence against any individual, but said he could not shut out from his mind that "even more than the finger of suspicion" pointed to Frederick Baker as the perpetrator of the deed. The jury agreed. They retired for fifteen minutes, then returned a verdict of wilful murder against Baker. He was then brought back into the court and formally committed to Winchester jail to await his trial at the next Hampshire Assizes. The day's drama, though, was not yet over.

"The prisoner," reported the *Hampshire Chronicle*, "did not betray the least sign of emotion at hearing this result, and was thereupon taken out of the room. He appeared very much disturbed, however, by the groans and remarks of the people who gathered outside the inn, where a determined attempt was made by an infuriated mob to 'lynch' the wretched man. Large bodies both of men and women posted themselves around the inn where the inquest was held and the lock-up, and two hours elapsed before it was deemed safe to attempt the removal of the prisoner. Baker was smuggled out at the back of the house and, surrounded by policemen, had to run at the top of his speed in order to reach the prison before the crowd which, having detected the manoeuvre, followed also at a racing pace, uttering the fiercest threats and the most hideous yells. The culprit himself escaped but several of the police suffered from the missiles hurled at him."

The next day, Wednesday, the remains of Fanny Adams were interred at Alton cemetery. A large crowd gathered for the funeral of the town's first murder victim in living memory.

Next day, Baker arrived at Alton town hall for his appearance before the local magistrates. He travelled from the police station to the town hall by horse and fly and his arrival was greeted with a chorus of groans and hisses from the large crowd. Baker appeared "greatly alarmed at the feelings expressed towards him" as police officers hustled him up the steps to the justice room, where his handcuffs were removed. The courtroom doors were then thrown open and in a few

Frederick Baker as portrayed by the *Illustrated Police News*.

A contemporary illustration showing Fanny's abduction.

The girl's head is severed.

James Gates makes his gruesome discovery.

moments the room was "densely crowded" while the street outside was "thronged by persons who could not obtain admission". Baker's self-possession gradually returned but throughout the hearing he looked "much careworn" as a "clammy perspiration suffused his countenance".

Much of the evidence heard by the magistrates was identical to that given at the inquest. George and Harriet Adams again had to endure the ordeal of speaking from the witness stand and both appeared in a pitiful state. Fannys father looked "painfully agitated" and answered questions concerning the identification of his daughter's remains in a "frenzied tone".

"He could not stand still," reported the *Hampshire Chronicle*. "Looking vacantly at the prisoner, he wandered to and fro – now passing his hands over the crown of his head, now clasping his hands together, and now wiping away the tears that rolled down his cheeks. After he had given his evidence he seated himself a short distance from the prisoner, and placing his head between his hands he tried, but in vain, to suppress his emotion."

Harriet Adams entered the courtroom supported by the arm of an elder daughter and appeared "feeble with grief".

"When called upon to identify the clothing of her child the scene became one of the most heartrending description," the newspaper went on. "Superintendent Cheyney placed the clothing, which was torn into rags and saturated with blood, on the floor. The poor woman feared to gaze upon them, and while she was making an effort to do so, her unhappy husband raised his head and gazing for some moments on the tattered clothing, he turned towards the prisoner and said: 'You are a villain, indeed!' The prisoner sat all the while with his eyes cast down, and did not in the least appear to notice this remark. The poor woman, at the conclusion of her evidence, seated herself by the side of her husband, but in a short time afterwards she, with two or three of their young children, left the court."

After all the prosecution evidence had been given, Baker said he wanted to call Mr French, a fellow clerk, as a witness, but not at the present hearing.

"I am not anxious to answer the charge at present. I am as innocent as on the day I was born," he added.

As he was removed from the building, the mob outside "hooted and con-ducted themselves in a most threatening manner". On reaching the safety of his cell at the police station, Baker commented: "I'm glad to get back here again. That's a very unpleasant affair over."

That evening, Baker was taken to the county jail at Winchester to await his trial at the assizes three months later. Again a large crowd greeted him as he left the police station; many "rushed after the cab" as it ascended the Romsey Road, throwing stones and shouting threats and abuse.

The long delay before the start of Baker's trial gave the newspapers the opportunity to investigate his past and speculate about his mental condition. They described him as a man of sallow complexion, 5 feet 4 inches tall and weighing 8 stone 10 pounds, who looked much younger than his 29 years. He came originally from Guildford where, according to the *West Surrey Times*, he was known as a man of "considerable intelligence" with habits "of the most dissipated character".

"He was," reported the *Hampshire Chronicle* in a story apparently based on the material already published by the Surrey paper, "for some time secretary of the Guildford Institute Debating Society, but his irregular habits induced the committee to request him to resign from office. His animal and bibulous propensities during the last three or four years were a matter of common remark in Guildford, and he was looked upon as a 'ne'er do weel', past all hope of reformation."

The report continues: "Notwithstanding his profligate habits, he was a professor of religion and partook regularly of the sacrament at Trinity Church. There is no doubt that he was carefully brought up and instructed in the truths of religion by pious parents, and until four years since, he was a very pious, steady young man. At that time he was paying his addresses, and was engaged to be married, to a highly respectable young person, who was in the service of Mrs Haydon as a lady's maid; but his advances were suddenly checked by certain communications which some persons thought it their duty to make to the young woman's parents. The young girl's brother also interfered, and the match was broken off. Young Baker was excessively indignant at this intervention, and talked loudly about actions for slander and the like, but of course nothing came of them."

From this time on, it seemed, Baker was a changed man. He gave way to drunkenness and other vices, adopted a reckless attitude, and "seemed to have little regard either for character or appearances". He was rumoured to be connected with an organization called the Guildford Guys, and to have "shared in their most dangerous proceedings".

After moving to Alton, and about two months before the death of Fanny Adams, Baker wrote to a Mr Phillips, whom he knew through the debating society at Guildford, claiming that he had entirely reformed – that he abstained from drink and went to bed at 11 o'clock and rose at 7. He added that his employers were very kind to him and that he spent his spare time in boating and reading good authors. He regularly attended church and experienced great comfort from the ministrations of an excellent and devoted clergyman. He felt much happier in his mind since he had altered his course and he was assured that there was a bright future for him.

A month later, in a letter to another friend, Baker wrote: "My quiet life here at Alton has enabled me to reflect upon the errors of my past life. I have quite reformed. I drink little, go to bed early, and do not neglect my Sabbath duties. I often think of my foolish conduct at Guildford, but I have prayed to God for his grace, and I now feel that a better course is open to me. I am very happy here and my employers are exceedingly kind to me. Remember me to all old friends, and tell them that Fred Baker is not now a drunken sot, but, by God's grace, a steady, respectable man. This is a quiet old town, and does not offer the temptations of Guildford. I know that you will be glad to hear of your old friend, and that is why I write."

The *Hampshire Chronicle* did not believe any of this. It maintained that all the while at Alton, Baker had been "pursuing a course of secret vice and dissipation".

Several newspapers carried reports during September suggesting that Baker, during his time at Guildford, had been responsible for the murder of a little girl at Shere in Surrey. One James Longhurst had recently been executed for that murder, but he had protested his innocence to the end. However, the *Hampshire Chronicle*, lofty as ever, concluded on September 28 that "on examination this appears to be a mere random supposition based upon a very imperfect knowledge of the facts connected with the murder at Shere".

As the weeks passed, the initial excitement stirred up by Fanny's horrific death began to subside, but in early October some new evidence restored the level of public interest almost to its former level.

"During the past week," the *Hampshire Chronicle* reported, "some additional facts have been brought to light in relation to this horrible tragedy, which lead to the belief that the prisoner Baker will be clearly and conclusively connected with the crime with which he stands charged. From a statement made by a little boy, whose parents reside near those of the deceased girl, it seems that the details of the murder are likely to receive a fuller revelation at the trial of the prisoner than has yet been given. The boy states that about two o'clock on the day of the murder he was passing towards the Hollows when he saw the prisoner leave the hop garden, his hands and clothes saturated with blood, and walk to the brook where, stooping down, he washed his hands. He then took a handkerchief from his pocket and wiped his breast."

As soon as the man realized he was being watched, he sternly told the boy to go home and, when he did not immediately comply, repeated the command. Then he again rinsed his hands in the brook before walking away towards the turnpike road, where he was seen by the toll-keeper. The boy subsequently told his mother what he had seen but for some reason she chose to keep it to herself until, in early October, she let it slip during a conversation in a pub.

On October 19, the *Chronicle* carried a further progress report on the police investigation and preparations for the trial. A minute examination of Frederick Baker's knives, clothes, and other possessions had by this time been carried out by Professor Taylor, of Guy's Hospital, who had confirmed that the blood on them was human blood. Police had also carried out a thorough but unsuccessful search of the hop field and surrounding area in the hope of finding another knife or knives or the child's breastbone, which was still missing.

As to Baker himself, the *Chronicle* asserted that his behaviour since his committal to Winchester Prison had been "anything but reserved". "He is very talkative to the warders," said the report, "but more especially to the chaplain, and is attentive to his religious duties. He seldom complains. Once when he did so, at not having sufficient exercise, he was told to walk faster, which he acted upon, but made no reply. He frequently refers to the murder and observes that his own conscience is quite clear. He wonders who the guilty party was and expresses a hope that whoever he was, he will be found out. He possesses an excellent appetite and sleeps well, which is rather remarkable considering that while under arrest at Alton, he shuddered at the sight of meat in any shape and was very much disturbed in his sleep. So strange was his conduct that a strict watch was placed over him as a precaution against his committing suicide."

Baker's trial began at 9.30 a.m. on the first Thursday in December 1867 amid immense public interest. From an early hour, all approaches to the Assize Court were beseiged by crowds hoping to gain admission to the courtroom. The opening of the proceedings was delayed and those unable to gain admission made so much noise that the judge, Mr Justice Mellor, threatened to jail anyone contributing to the disturbance. Baker himself walked to the court unnoticed by the public, thanks to the special and highly secret arrangements of the local police. The route taken was via Battery House, passing Winchester Cemetery and crossing the Barrack parade ground to enter the court by a back door.

Montague Bere, opening for the prosecution, spoke of the publicity the case

Right: Fanny Adams' gravestone in Alton Cemetery. *(Photo: Bob Richardson)*

SACRED
TO THE MEMORY OF
FANNY ADAMS
AGED 8 YEARS AND 4 MONTHS.
WHO WAS CRUELLY MURDERED
ON SATURDAY AUG 24TH 1867.

FEAR NOT THEM WHICH KILL THE BODY BUT
ARE NOT ABLE TO KILL THE SOUL BUT RATHER
FEAR HIM WHICH IS ABLE TO DESTROY BOTH
SOUL AND BODY IN HELL. Matthew 10 V28

THIS STONE WAS ERECTED BY VOLUNTARY SUBSCRIPTION

Below: The parents of Fanny Adams in later life.

had already attracted and asked the jury to disregard anything they may have heard or read outside the courtroom and be guided in their deliberations solely by the evidence that would be put before them. He then summarized the prosecution evidence before calling a large number of witnesses, most of whom were testifying for the third time, having already given their accounts at the inquest and the magisterial hearing at Alton. One of the few new witnesses was seven-year-old Alfred Vince, the little boy whose story had already been told in part in the *Chronicle*. He described seeing a man come out of the Hollow and wash his hands in the stream at a spot where boys often bathed. He said that the man had afterward run after him. He also saw Mrs Gardener and Emma Smith speak to the man. Under cross-examination, he agreed that when he was taken to an identity parade at the county prison, he passed by the prisoner at first and only recognized him after his mother had given him a nudge.

The exhibits produced in court included a stone alleged by the prosecution to be the weapon used to hit Fanny on the head. Painter William Walker, who found the piece of flint in the hop garden, said it was covered with blood and hair. He took it home and put in in a window.

The court adjourned at 6 p.m. The final prosecution witnesses – including Professor Taylor and Dr Leslie – were heard when the case resumed next morning.

In his two-hour opening speech, the defence counsel, Carter, maintained that the prosecution had failed to prove that his client was the killer of Fanny Adams. There was, he claimed, no evidence of motive and Baker had always maintained his innocence; the facts also showed Baker "in so many places at once that he could not have been where the murder was committed unless he possessed ubiquity"; and it was hard to believe that the small knife produced in court was the instrument that had been used to dismember a body. As a second line of defence, said Mr Carter, he would offer evidence about Baker's state of mind to show that he could not be held responsible for his actions.

Carter then called the defendant's father, Frederick Baker senior, who said his son had been backward as a child and had suffered very bad health up to the age of twelve. His "nervous system" was always bad. He had headaches, often accompanied by sickness. He was also subject to frequent nosebleeds. At the age of sixteen he had typhus fever, after which he continued complaining of his head. Even after he started work, he used to come home and say that his office duties were more than he could bear and he would often burst out crying. Nevertheless he became a director of a penny savings bank, was a Sunday school teacher for ten years, and did not touch alcohol until he was twenty-six. In 1864 he became engaged to a young woman and the engagement continued until the beginning of 1865.

Mary Baker, the defendant's elder sister, said the ending of her brother's love affair had a very bad effect on him. He became unhappy and despondent and said several times that he would destroy himself. He told her that he had once tried to kill himself but a young man had saved him.

More evidence about Baker's mental condition came from John Davis, a bricklayer and former police sergeant, who knew him well and was sometimes accompanied by Baker for an hour or two while pounding his beat. He said Baker's conduct was sometimes "peculiar" and he would make grim faces and leave. He would walk in a very excited and rapid manner about the town, sometimes up to one or two in the morning. Once he saw Baker heading for the river and seized him as he was rushing along and took him home. On this occasion, Baker told him he would "do something to be talked about".

Baker's landlady at Alton, Sarah Kingston, said her lodger always appeared very dull and low in spirits and also "appeared wild". She noticed this particularly on August 24. But under cross-examination, she denied that he was in the habit of drinking, adding that she saw him the worse for liquor on only one occasion. He usually arrived home early and went to bed at ten.

From two family doctors, the jury heard of other instances of insanity in Baker's family. His cousin, Richard Rowe, of Alton, was "very violent and of homicidal tendency" and was currently in the Fareham Lunatic Asylum, having been in other asylums on four previous occasions. He was "only prevented by restraint from carrying out his tendencies", said Rowe's doctor, William Curtis.

Baker's father, too, had, four years before, had an "attack of acute mania and was violent". He tried to strike his daughter with a poker and, on another occasion, attacked his son and daughter, whom he thought were trying to poison him. And according to the Bakers' family doctor, Dr Taylor, of Guildford, the defendant himself was "very nervous and sensitive" and showed "some marks tending to insanity".

"A year or two before he left Guildford, I noticed a great difference in his manner," Dr Taylor told the court. "He always was somewhat weak-minded, which would be increased by the taint of insanity in the family. He changed from being a very weak, inoffensive man to something swaggering, which had the look of intemperance."

In his summing up, Mr Justice Mellor said the case was one of the most remarkable he had tried, depending as it did almost exclusively on presumptive evidence arising from the conduct of the prisoner, and from an entry in his diary. He spoke for two hours and the jury retired at seven o'clock after two long days of evidence. When they returned after just fifteen minutes, the atmosphere was tense and the silence profound.

"Do you find the prisoner guilty or not guilty?" asked the Clerk of Arraigns.

"Guilty," the foreman replied.

The *Hampshire Chronicle* reported: "The prisoner was slightly affected by the verdict. His countenance indicated a momentary depression, and he nervously squeezed his hands together. The verdict was carried into the body of the hall immediately, and there was a sudden commotion apparent. The prisoner was then asked if he had anything to say why sentence of death should not be passed upon him, and making no reply, his lordship put on the black cap and addressed him in the most solemn and impressive manner."

The judge told Baker that his crime was one "committed under circumstances rarely parallelled in the history of this country". He continued: "For some purpose, probably the gratification of your lust, you carried that unfortunate child into the hop-garden and there – whether you effected your purpose or not is only known to yourself and your Maker – you brutally murdered her, and afterwards dreadfully mutilated and dismembered her body, with the view, probably, of destroying all possibility of identity, and probably for the purposes of concealment."

He said the crime was a "shock to common humanity" and urged Baker to prepare himself for his dread account, for his time on earth was short and he must shortly appear before "the Searcher of all hearts".

"During this terrible ordeal, heightened to the highest solemnity by the earnestness of the Judge throughout, and which visibly affected, even to emotion, many in court, the prisoner appeared scarcely moved," reported the *Chronicle*. "He stood erect, with his hands hanging down clutched in front, and, turning calmly round, walked slowly away from the dock."

Baker's execution was fixed for Tuesday December 24 and no sooner had the date been announced than rumours began to circulate that a respite had been granted. The stories caused much alarm in and around Alton, where the antipathy to Baker was such that a petition calling on the Home Secretary to commute the death sentence attracted but a single signature, everyone other than its initiator having refused to sign it. Feelings were running so high that the Vicar of Alton, the Rev O. A. Hodges, felt it necessary to declare publicly that,

A contemporary front page montage of Fred Baker's last hours and execution.

contrary to another rumour, he had neither signed the document himself nor urged George and Harriet Adams to do so.

The rumours concerning a possible stay of execution were untrue, as also were claims that since the trial, Baker had become "reserved and refuses his meals" and that he was "excited and paces his cell with rapid and restless steps".

"We have reason to know," the *Chronicle* assured its readers, "that all such reports are unfounded and that on the contrary he is respectful and attentive to all who are engaged in attending upon him and that in no instance has he manifested any unbecoming conduct." Baker's "respectful" behaviour extended to the parents of his victim, to whom, on his own initiative, he wrote a letter, delivered to them a few days before his execution. In it he confessed that he had committed the crime "in an unguarded hour, and not with malice aforethought". He expressed his deep sorrow and sought their forgiveness. He said that he had killed Fanny because he was "enraged at her crying, but it was done without a pain or struggle", and he denied that he had violated, or even tried to violate, the child.

The letter reached Mr and Mrs Adams through the prison chaplain, the Rev. Foster Rogers, and the vicar of Alton, the Rev. Hodges. The couple immediately made known their relief at the confession and their willingness to forgive their daughter's killer, adding, however, that their satisfaction would have been greater and their forgiveness more readily given if he had also revealed where he had hidden the missing portion of the girl's body, which they hoped he would yet do before his execution.

Baker was reported to have made additional confessions in his prison cell in which he stated that Fanny Adams was hanging head down from his shoulder in the hop-garden and struggling to get away and that he stuck a knife into her throat. "The blood flowed outwards from him and he dropped her on the ground. She was dead almost instantly. Bewildered, but not insane, as he himself admitted, he immediately decapitated her, without considering why he did so." The mutilation was said to have been an afterthought. Baker felt that he "must become saturated with blood and experienced no revulsion" while engaged in carving the little girl's body into twenty pieces. For some time he walked about with her heart, still smoking hot, in his hand and threw it into a field when he heard someone approaching.

On the night before his execution, Baker retired at 11 o'clock. At 5 o'clock next morning, he rose and was visited by the Rev. Rogers. He took breakfast at 7 o'clock and continued in conversation with the chaplain until 7.55, when the prison bell began to toll. Outside the county jail, a crowd of several thousand had already gathered to await his death.

"Some hundreds of the working classes of the city," reported the *Chronicle*, "and many by early trains from Southampton and Portsmouth, a few shop-keepers, a large proportion of women and a small sprinkling of nondescripts made up a concourse of not less than 5,000 persons, who stood in the grey dawn gazing at the hideous machine which overtopped the noble and massive portals of the county jail. It was a most orderly mob."

As the clock struck eight, the prisoner, accompanied by the chaplain, the under-sheriff, the surgeon, the deputy governor, and warders, proceeded to the scaffold, where his arrival was greeted by a solemn silence from the crowd. The distance covered was 200 yards and included a flight of 190 stone steps, but Baker negotiated it all with a firm and unfaltering step.

"The pinioning room," said the *Chronicle*, "is just below the scaffold, and the culprit with great composure submitted to this trying ordeal to which he was subjected by Calcraft. He ascended the remaining steps to the scaffold with great firmness and listened with attention and responded with fervour to the pious ministrations of the chaplain. The fatal bolt was then drawn by Calcraft and after a few convulsive struggles the unhappy criminal ceased to exist."

Frederick Baker was the last person to be hanged publicly at Winchester, and one of the last in England, where executions ceased to be a public spectacle in 1868. His crime, which enraged a town and shocked a nation, turned him into one of the most notorious criminals of his time. Yet, curiously, it is his victim, not he, who has become a household name. The expression "Sweet Fanny Adams", meaning "sweet nothing" or "nothing at all", owes its origin to the gruesome fate of Baker's tragic victim and to the morbid humour of Queen Victoria's navy. The navy adopted Fanny's name as a synonym for tinned mutton, which first appeared in their rations at this time. As a consequence, the phrase came to mean "anything worthless" and eventually "nothing at all".

5
THE COACHMAN'S CONQUEST

The murder of Elsie Matthews in 1896

A low mist hung over Winchester at dawn on Tuesday July 21, 1896, but it was one of those mists that signal the imminent arrival of something better. By 7.30, it had been dispelled by the rising sun and the city was enjoying the early stages of a glorious summer's day. For three men within the walls of the county jail, however, the weather was of no consequence. For them, there was little more than thirty minutes of life remaining. By the time the sun reached its zenith, their corpses would be interred in a shared grave outside the prison's northwest wing.

One of the trio was Samuel Edward Smith, a private in the 4th Battalion the King's Royal Rifles, stationed at the North Camp, Aldershot. On May 28, he had walked into a barrack room where several other soldiers were peeling potatoes for dinner, placed his rifle against his hip, and fired. One of the spud-bashers, Corporal Robert Payne, was hit in the neck and fell dying on the floor. Smith was immediately arrested, at which he remarked: "I have done it, and I meant to do it."

It was soon established that Smith had sworn to take revenge on Payne, who had reported him for being drunk several weeks earlier. At his trial for murder, he "preserved a cool and careless demeanour" and initially entered a guilty plea before changing it to not guilty on the advice of his counsel. But it took a jury only a few minutes to decide that he was guilty and, as sentence of death was passed, Smith reacted "without a word, and left the dock in the same indifferent manner".

Frederick Burden, aged 24, was far from indifferent about his impending fate. On his last night before the executions he was restless and troubled in his sleep. Burden's crime was the murder of his lover, the inaptly-named Angelina Faithfull, at their home in Brooklyn Road (now Belgrave Road), Southampton. The two had had a stormy relationship and Angelina, a married woman and an alcoholic, had already accused him of trying to kill her by both poisoning and strangulation. Then, on February 19, 1896, she was found dead, a razor blade in her hand and her throat slit from ear to ear. It appeared that the killer had tried to make the crime look like suicide but medical experts said the injuries could not possibly have been self-inflicted. Burden had disappeared but was arrested two days later and, despite protesting his innocence, was convicted and sentenced to death.

But it was the third member of the trio, 32-year-old Philip Matthews, whose offence had caused by far the greatest sensation at the Hampshire Summer Assizes of 1896 and the weeks and months leading up to them. His was a story of betrayal and intended bigamy, of deceit and of death. It sent shock waves around the region and eclipsed other topics of conversation in Portsmouth and district for some time.

According to medical practitioner Dr Piggott, of Teignmouth, Devon, who employed Matthews as a coachman for almost ten years, he was a fundamentally honest, caring person. "He is a man of excellent character and I found him scrupulously honest," Dr Piggott told a judge and jury following Matthews' arrest.

Matthews' problems began early in 1892, when he and his wife contracted influenza. Both suffered very badly from the illness and to Mrs Matthews it proved fatal. She died in February of that year, leaving her husband to bring up their baby daughter, Elsie Gertrude, born the previous July. Matthews and Elsie continued to live at The Lawn, a house rented for them by Dr Piggott. But the coachman was devastated by the tragedy.

"His grief at the death of his wife was extravagant," Dr Piggott recalled. "He seemed strange in his mind and talked of committing suicide." He always displayed "great attachment" for the child and treated her "very kindly". But he also displayed symptoms of trouble with his nervous system, including an involuntary jerking of the knee.

Six months after his wife's death, Matthews married again. His second wife, whom he had known since 1887, was called Maria. She cared well for her husband and step-daughter and for some time the family lived happily together. But then Matthews became friendly with Charlotte Maloney, a young parlour-maid in service at Miss Barclay's boarding house at West Lawn, Teignmouth. Matthews had cause to visit West Lawn occasionally and he first met Charlotte – whom he came to know as Lottie – soon after she arrived there from her home in Portsmouth in April 1895. Lottie was a tall, good-looking girl and the attraction was strong and mutual. As a contemporary journalist later put it, Matthews became "madly infatuated" with her, and she was "not indifferent" to him.

To further his cause, Matthews told Lottie that although Maria had been introduced to her as Mrs Matthews, she was not his legal wife and he was really a single man and free to marry her. Little Elsie, he added, was not his daughter but Maria's illegitimate child. Matthews also told Lottie tempting stories about impending wealth and a forthcoming inheritance. Their friendship blossomed and their interest in each other did not escape Maria's attention. Not surprisingly, her marriage to Matthews began to founder. Quarrels between the couple became commonplace and soon a separation was being talked about. Maria repeatedly reminded her husband that she was not little Elsie's natural mother and that she was not prepared to continue looking after the girl if he went to live with another woman. But Matthews was undeterred.

Things reached a head at Easter 1896. On March 23, Matthews took a train to Portsmouth, where he called at Lottie's mother's house in St Mary's Crescent, Kingston, and introduced himself as Philip Burt, "Lottie's lover". Then he went to Salisbury, where he met Lottie by arrangement. While in Salisbury he called at the Registry Office and applied for a special licence to marry there two days later, on March 25. He and Lottie then travelled on to Portsmouth, where they had some wedding cards printed, in a dainty and fashionable style, announcing the marriage of Lottie Maloney to Philip Burt. These were sent by Lottie to her friends and relations in the area. The couple also visited Lottie's mother, where Matthews reintroduced himself as the young woman's husband. Then they went to the Speedwell Hotel, where they stayed as man and wife until April 1. On the morning of April 2, they returned to Teignmouth.

Matthews had already terminated his employment with Dr Piggott and on April 3, which was Good Friday, he visited the doctor to explain what was happening. He met Lottie again next day, in Exeter, where he told her that Maria was threatening to put Elsie in the workhouse. Then he and Lottie went back to Portsmouth, spending one night at the Victoria Hotel, Landport, and a second – Easter Sunday night – at Lottie's mother's house. Then, at 4.45 on Easter

Monday morning, Matthews left for Teignmouth once again, saying that he was going to settle some money matters.

On Easter Monday, Matthews left his home at Teignmouth for the last time. He was seen carrying Elsie under one arm and a paper parcel under the other. He told his landlord that he was going to take the little girl to a place where she would be cared for. The landlord told the departing coachman that if Maria Matthews had been his sister, he would "knock your bloody head off!"

Late that night, 150 miles away in Hampshire, the sound of a child screaming set the dogs barking at Baffins Farm, Copnor, on Portsea Island. The screams were followed a few seconds later by a splash. The following day a farmworker found the body of a girl, "respectably attired" and thought to be aged about seven, in a ditch adjoining a farm road at Copnor. She was fully clothed and clean linen had been placed neatly under her head and brown paper at her feet. Her bib bore the name "Elsie" and the name "Piggott" appeared on her underclothing.

"As the result of the post mortem examination, the police are working on the theory that she was strangled," the *Hampshire Chronicle* reported later. "The spot where the body was found was divided only by a ditch and an occupation road from Baffins Pond, a large sheet of water in front of the farmhouse, and several hours were spent on Wednesday afternoon in dragging the pond, but the only find was a white silk brush and comb bag, which it is surmised belonged to the deceased child. A signalman at an adjacent level crossing identified the girl as the one who passed through the railway gates on Monday afternoon and some other people speak of having seen her in the neighbourhood on Monday with a man and a woman."

Philip Matthews was arrested on the Thursday, April 9, at the Lamb Inn, Fareham. He told the arresting officer that he had not murdered the child but that "the poor little thing" had died of fright after hearing dogs barking. Later he added: "I have had a lot of trouble lately, and have been haunted. My mind has not been very well lately but it is better today."

Six days later, still in custody, he sat beside his solicitor as an inquest jury considered the circumstances surrounding the death of Elsie Gertrude Matthews, aged four-and-three-quarters. Maria Matthews was also present, as was Lottie Maloney.

After describing the breakdown of her marriage following the quarrels she had with her husband over his relationship with Lottie, Maria said she had received a telegram from him on the afternoon of Tuesday April 7, saying: "Safe in

London, writing long letter. Phil." She noticed, though, that the telegram had been despatched from Botley, between Southampton and Portsmouth, and next day she received a letter from her husband bearing the Botley postmark.

"Dear Maria," he wrote. "After what passed yesterday, you must know how I feel. I hear you saying, 'Now, you are not in your right mind,' but I am sometimes, and sometimes not. What am I doing this morning? I find myself where I have never been before. Can I hope once more to bear my good name, which once was so dear to me? It is those girls at Teignmouth who have ruined me, for you know they like to crush people. Do as I ask you, Maria: spare Lottie, who, as you know, has been led by me. I have a lot of trouble to go through. Shall I ever survive it? Yes, I must, for the sake of others who I have wronged. I know you would not crush me of your own free will, and I honour you for it, but all seems dark and dreary, and I fear will never be right again. I left Elsie looking so happy, and I hope I may see you happy. If prayers and good wishes can help you, I send you abundance. I cannot come back to you, I have only a few shillings, given me by a good friend. I hear those Teignmouth jeers now, but I hope to laugh at them. I will do my best to return. I am asking the master to send me some money to come back with."

The letter ended abruptly at this point but an enclosure added: "Please pardon me. I know you will do all you can for Elsie. Ask the doctor to do his best, which I'm sure he will. May God help you in all your troubles. Those who know me from my birth will be surprised. My last prayer is, may you and Elsie be happy."

Scrawled across the paper was the word "Goodbye".

Pressed as to whether she had anything more to tell the inquest, Maria Matthews, after some hesitation, said her husband had told her that he was married to another woman before Elsie's mother and that that woman was still alive. She believed her name to be Cowley and that last Christmas she was living at Dawlish. She said Matthews had also stated that he was married to Lottie Maloney.

When the inquest was resumed the following day, Dr Piggott was among those who took the stand, and he produced several messages that Matthews had sent to him. In one, which the doctor had received on April 7, Matthews described himself as penniless and homeless. In a telegram addressed from Fareham that arrived on April 8, he asked his former employer to send him enough money to pay his fare home to Teignmouth. On April 9 another letter came through Dr Piggott's letter box asking for 11 shillings. The letters spoke of the trouble the "jeers of the Teignmouth people" had caused Matthews.

The inquest jury returned a verdict of wilful murder against Matthews, who was committed on the coroner's warrant to take his trial at the Winchester Assizes. The trial was held on Friday June 26, 1896, and Matthews, who had served in the army before becoming a coachman, had a "somewhat military appearance" as he stood in the dock. But his composure cracked as the charge of murdering his own daughter was read out. Tears filled his eyes as he said in a broken voice: "Not guilty."

The prosecution witnesses included Chief Petty Officer Edward Mills, of H.M.S. *Victory*, who said he and his wife had travelled in the same compartment as Matthews on a train journey from Exeter to Portsmouth on Easter Monday. Matthews was accompanied by a small child, whom he treated kindly and held to his breast during the journey. Mills said that at Yeovil Matthews bought the child some milk. Later Mrs Mills gave her an apple, which Matthews peeled for her. Mills said Matthews started to alight from the train at Cosham but it moved off and, saying that the next station would do, he got out at Fratton instead.

Dr Piggott was also among the witnesses, as was Lottie Maloney. Clothed in a fawn-coloured dress and jacket, with a sailor hat and white fall or veil, and wearing gold-rimmed spectacles, the coachman's mistress cut an elegant figure as she took the stand. She appeared cool and self-possessed as she told the court about her first meeting with Matthews, about the introduction to Maria, about Matthews' claim that Maria was not his wife. She told of how their friendship grew, of her belief that he was a single man, of how the "intimacy" between them culminated in their elopement and their stay as man and wife at a Portsmouth hotel. Even at this point, Lottie managed to maintain her composure, and it was only when her story reached the point of her last, brief meeting with Matthews two days before his arrest that she finally broke.

"He came about ten on the Tuesday morning and I spoke to him in the kitchen at my mother's house," said Lottie. "He was wearing a blue suit and had a hard hat. I was rather struck with his appearance. He seemed so strange. I said I was surprised to see him back because he'd said he should not be back till the Tuesday night. He said he must come and see me before he went away but then he must be off again. He stayed about ten minutes, then he put on a cap and a dust coat over his other coat and he went away. I didn't see him again till he was in custody."

At this point in her evidence, Lottie burst into tears and was given a chair in the witness box. She then revealed that the child's hairbrush and bag found in Baffin's Pond were a Christmas present from her to little Elsie.

"I was very fond of the child myself," she said.

Asked if, in the event of her continuing to live with Matthews, she would have had any objection to Elsie living with them, she replied: "It was never suggested to me."

Potentially crucial evidence came from two witnesses who saw Matthews in the early hours of that Tuesday, April 7, a few hours before Elsie's body was discovered. One of the witnesses was William Stares, the signalman at Copnor Crossing, who said that at 1.40 a.m. he saw a man he now recognized as Matthews and had a brief conversation with him about where he was going. The other was Lottie's mother, Charlotte Jane Maloney, who said Matthews knocked on the window at 4.10 a.m. and she got up to let him in.

"He looked much worried," she recalled. "He had some lemonade and biscuit but he didn't go into the room where my daughter was. He stayed only ten minutes in the house and then said, 'I must be off.' He did not say where to but he did go. I saw him again about a quarter-past-ten the same morning."

Like Lottie Maloney, Matthews remained composed and collected for most of the hearing, the only sign of nervousness being his constant scribbling of notes which he passed through the prison warders to his solicitor. But when the injuries to Elsie were described, and a photograph of his dead daughter was produced, he was visibly moved. He wiped tears from his eyes as police surgeon Dr L. Maybury spoke of finding three marks on the girl's neck which he believed were caused by a person's fingers.

"He said the child died from asphyxia by throttling," said the *Hampshire Chronicle* in its report on the trial. "The marks on the throat were quite sufficient to account for death by such means. In addition to the marks on the throat, there were signs within the body to confirm his opinion – the state of the heart, the lungs, the bronchial tubes, the congestion of the brain and the internal organs. It was in his opinion not the case that the child had died from fright from hearing a dog bark (as prisoner had suggested) – if the child had died from fright the body would have been pale, he should not have expected to have found the heart and brain in the state they were."

The evidence against Matthews appeared to be overwhelming but the coach-man and his lawyers still clung to the hope, albeit an increasingly faint one, that they might be able to convince the jury that Elsie's death was an accident. But even that hope was virtually dashed when a temporary warder at Kingston Prison, John Hornby, took the stand. He testified that on April 25, Matthews passed a bundle of clothes out of his cell with a request that they be sent to Miss

Copnor Crossing, where the signalman spoke to Philip Matthews.

Maloney. Hornby examined the bundle and found an envelope which he handed to the chief warder.

The letter in the envelope was addressed to "My dearest Lottie". In it, amid fairly incoherent protestations of love, Matthews told, damningly, how he had decided to take Elsie's life, then Lottie's, then his own. He declared that he would do anything for Lottie's sake, "dearest, best of all", and he asked her not to hesitate to say what she thought best. There were more "effusive expressions", said the *Hampshire Chronicle*, and the letter concluded, "Ever yours in life and death", a supplementary note being signed "Your loving boy, Phil".

Mr Barnes, for the defence, told the jury that although Matthews had done wrong in leaving his wife and going off with Charlotte Maloney, the court was not a court of morals. He then advanced a new theory concerning the cause of Elsie's death. He suggested that, not wishing to disturb Lottie's mother at 1.30 in the morning, Matthews had laid down with the child and, pressing her to him, had accidentally smothered her in his sleep.

But Mr Barnes' task was a near–impossible one and it took the jury only fifteen minutes to reach the unanimous conclusion that Matthews was guilty of murdering his daughter. Asked if he had anything to say before sentence was passed, the prisoner replied: "I am not guilty. I am only sorry I cannot be allowed to explain where I was between 4 and 10 o'clock."

Maria Matthews remained in court to witness the final, dramatic moments of the trial but Lottie Maloney stayed in the waiting room. It was in solemn and at times almost broken tones that Mr Justice Day implored Matthews to "dismiss from your mind all thought of this world and devote yourself for preparation for the next". Matthews listened "attentively and with a fair amount of composure" as the judge sentenced him to death. Before being led from the dock, he commented: "I am glad I am going where my child is."

Matthews was tried on Friday June 26 and Samuel Smith on June 27 but Frederick Burden's trial was held over until the following week, which had the effect of extending the period of grace usually granted to condemned prisoners by one week for all three men. Following his conviction, Matthews was driven back to the prison not in the usual prison van but in a cab. On arrival he was taken to the condemned cell, where he was stripped and searched before being left alone with two warders. Regulations decreed that from the moment the death sentence was passed, a condemned man must not set eyes on another prisoner, and elaborate precautions were taken to ensure that the doomed trio were not observed even by each other whenever they moved around the prison corridors.

"The condemned man attends the ordinary daily service in the prison chapel, but he proceeds there accompanied only by the watching warders, and the seating of the chapel admits of his being brought in alone, and placed wholly out of the sight of others, and he takes his daily airing in the exercise yard alone," said the *Hampshire Chronicle* in its report on the triple execution. "This has been the procedure as regards Matthews, Smith and Burden, and until the men were formed up in the fatal procession neither had seen the other. We believe Matthews and Burden took Communion together on the Sunday or the Monday but they were then screened off at different sides of the chapel. Of course the other prisoners cannot help knowing what is impending because their prayers are asked for the condemned, and the services, particularly on the last Sunday, are of a very solemn character."

The report continues: "The cells allotted for the condemned prisoners are situated in the centre of the prison, from which corridors branch off in four directions, somewhat in the fashion, as it has been described, of a cart-wheel. Matthews' cell was on the level above the main floor, from which it is approached by a short spiral iron staircase. On the same level and opposite Matthews' cell was that of the young rifleman Smith, and just below on the main corridor was the cell of Burden, the Southampton murderer."

Matthews' only visitor after his conviction was his wife, Maria, who came to see him the following day. But even during that visit Matthews could not resist bringing Lottie Maloney into the conversation repeatedly, causing his wife to threaten to leave the prison immediately if that was all he could talk about. In fact, she did bid a final farewell on that occasion and was never seen in Winchester again. Lottie also applied to visit her lover before she left Winchester after the trial, but "it was not convenient for her to do so, and she does not appear to have renewed her application". One of the last letters written by Matthews before he went to the scaffold was addressed to Lottie. Matthews was believed to have a mother and a brother or brothers living (he spoke in sorrowing terms of his mother) but they were presumed to be too far away to visit him.

Matthews, Smith and Burden were each watched night and day by two warders during the period leading up to their executions but conversation was not encouraged, particularly where it concerned their crimes.

"Books are provided from the prison library both for the prisoner and his watchers," the Chronicle tells us. "There is daily exercise and daily ministrations from the chaplain. A prisoner is allowed writing materials, but only within reasonable limits and no written matter passes the portals of the prison without the previous sanction of the Governor. If a condemned man wishes to indulge in columns of writing he must make use of his slate, and when he has filled both the sides of it the only course open to him is to clean his slate and start afresh. Of course no work, in the ordinary acceptation of the word, is engaged in – a prisoner in the eyes of the law is dead from the moment the Judge pronounces sentence. The time of a condemned person is occupied in reading, writing, devotions, exercise, eating, and sleeping."

Another custom was to allow condemned men to enjoy better food than their fellow inmates. For Matthews, Smith and Burden, the diet included white bread and butter and tea for breakfast, meat and potatoes for dinner, plus milk for Smith, a teetotaller, and beer for the other two. All three men had been smokers and they were each allowed two cigarettes while taking their daily exercise.

On the day fixed for the executions, the three men ate a light breakfast. The bell signalling the start of the prison day rang at 5.40 a.m. and the trio were then made ready to receive the chaplain. At 6 o'clock they were taken to the three cells nearest the execution shed. This practice had been introduced by the

Governor two years earlier in order to spare condemned prisoners the additional ordeal of an unnecessarily long walk to the place of execution.

The man whose duty it was to carry out the executions was a Bolton hairdresser and former Sunday-school teacher called James Billington, the chief hangman of England. It was his second triple execution in six weeks and on the previous occasion he had come close to making it a quadruple one by almost despatching his assistant as well. The incident happened at Newgate Prison in London on June 9 and the assistant executioner in question was a man named Warbrick. Because of fears that the men to be executed might struggle and resist, four warders had been posted on the scaffold and one of them obscured Warbrick from Billington's line of vision. Warbrick was still pinioning the feet of one of the men when Billington pulled the lever that opened the trapdoors, catapulting his assistant into the pit. Fortunately for Warbrick, he heard the bolt beneath being drawn and instinctively grabbed the legs of the man in front of him. Although he plunged head-first through the trap, he retained his hold to end up swinging safely below the feet of the three dead men.

Taking his chances as Billington's assistant on July 21 at Winchester was not Warbrick but a man named Wilkinson. Like Billington, he had a very ordinary "main" occupation (as an insurance agent) and, also like Billington, an ecclesiastical sideline (as a preacher). Both were described as "very moderate drinkers" and of a "religious turn of mind". Billington, a short, thick-set man, would have been paid £10 for his first victim at one session and £5 for every other one, plus his expenses, while Wilkinson, who was taller and slimmer, could expect to earn about £5.

The executioners arrived in the city at 4 o'clock the previous afternoon and satisfied themselves that the equipment was in working order before settling into their temporary quarters. Further checks were carried out next morning, when those watching the proceedings included four invited newsmen. For three of them – from the Press Association and the Central News Agency in London and a newspaper in the West Country – witnessing an execution was to be a new experience, but our man from the *Hampshire Chronicle* was an old hand, having seen "about a score of individuals pay the forfeit of their crimes".

Between 7.45 and 7.59, the reporters were able to watch the preparations – the arrival of the Governor, Under-Sheriff, and other officials, the inspection of the drop, the comparing of watches and the strapping of the prisoners' arms behind their backs by Billington and Wilkinson.

"Meanwhile, in the execution shed the pressmen find Chief Engineer Bryant in charge," writes the *Chronicle* man. "From the chains of the overhead beam hang the three ropes – stout hempen cords – the looped ends of which are encased in leather, and have a metal ring inserted so as to ensure the sure running of the noose. Our representative inquires, and is told the drop to be allowed Matthews and Smith is six feet, and Burden, being the lightest of the three men, is to be given three inches more. All the ropes hang at the same level above the platform, but looking up at the beam one sees the requisite length of rope is held in a loop at the top by a thin thread of cotton or silk, which will be broken by the fall of the body and allow the rope to run out. On the platform itself the executioner has chalked three T-shaped lines to indicate where he wishes the culprits to stand, and as the men's toes are to be at the top part of the T, their backs will be to the onlookers, but their faces towards the side on which Billington principally works. To each chalk mark is the initial letter of the man's surname, thus M B S. Smith, as the heaviest of the three men, being placed nearest the lever – which is like the handle of a signalman's points on the right hand side. Still the prison bell is tolling dolefully at slow intervals."

At less than a minute to eight, those in the execution shed heard the muffled tread of the approaching procession and the chaplain's voice uttering comforting passages from scripture. This time the procession included the three "culprits", as the reporters called them. Samuel Smith was dressed in a cheap, dark grey "Martini-Henry" suit of the type given to men on their discharge from the army, his dark green Rifle uniform having been returned to his regiment following his conviction.

"He has almost instinctively fallen into a military slow step, and he approaches the fatal drop with as much apparent unconcern as though he were marching to the parade ground," writes our *Chronicle* correspondent. "Burden's movement is different, and his face wears a half-agonised look. Matthews, again, walks steadily, though his face is pale. Burden and Matthews are attired as when on their trial, save that their necks are bared. The men are now on the drop, and Billington's actions have a rapidity about them that one who has not witnessed would find difficulty in believing from a written description. He straps Smith's legs near the ankles, throws off his cap, adjusts the noose around his neck, drawing the loop fairly taut, and then envelopes his head in a white calico bag. All this while Burden has turned his head, and is nervously watching Billington's movements, and when the hangman turns to the wretched man, and goes through a similar process with him, Burden is visibly shaking. Wilkinson having placed the leg straps around Matthews, steps off the platform, and removes the chain from the handle of the lever waiting by it in readiness for Billington. Before Billington comes to him with the noose and cap Matthews turns his body half-round, and bows with self-possession and in a respectful manner towards where the Governor and other prison officials are."

As the chaplain began to recite the Lord's Prayer, and several of the other onlookers joined in, Billington took a last hurried look over the men to see that all was as it should be.

"Then gliding, as it were, to the lever, Wilkinson steps away, and Billington pushes over the handle, which allows the doors to open, and the wretched culprits are launched into eternity before a third of the Lord's Prayer has been said, for there is no 'given signal' as some people fancy. The doors fall back against thick pads fixed to the wall to deaden the sound, but the shooting over of the bolts and the clatter of the opening doors are painfully audible to those whose nerves are already on the strain. The Chaplain breaks off at the point he had reached in the Lord's Prayer, and apparently prays in silence for a few minutes over the pit, and he then pronounces the Mosaic blessing... The men's heads are just below the level of the platform, and the bodies hang without a quiver at the end of the rope – the spinal column has been broken, and death for practical purposes has been instantaneous in each case. And it has now only just struck eight o'clock."

So ended the lives of three men whom fate had brought together in the worst circumstances, men whose only common factor was that they had each committed the ultimate crime. News that the executions had been satisfactorily carried out was immediately conveyed to the crowd of 200 people outside the prison gates by the unfurling of a black flag. Among those present to witness the moment was Samuel Smith's brother, also a soldier, whose face betrayed the "mental strain he was palpably undergoing". There were no friends or relatives of Philip Matthews in the crowd. His wife, Maria, was 150 miles away in Teignmouth, contemplating life as the widow of an unfaithful husband who had murdered his own daughter in an attempt to clear the way for a bigamous marriage. As for his lover, Lottie Maloney, she was less than thirty miles away in Portsmouth, preparing for life as the unmarried mother of a child whose father had been executed for murder several months before its birth.

6

THE POISONED PARTRIDGES

The death of Hubert Chevis in 1931

Hubert George Chevis was not a man who readily made enemies during his career as an officer in the Royal Artillery or, as far as is known, in his private life. According to a fellow officer in the regiment's 15th Light Battery, he was extremely popular with officers and men alike. He was not known to have any enemies and he and his wife, Frances, appeared to be happily married. It was Mrs Chevis's second marriage, her first husband being a Major Jackson of the Royal Army Veterinary Corps, by whom she had three children. For reasons which were never made public, that marriage ended in divorce – a relatively unusual occurrence in the 1920s – and in December 1930, Frances Jackson had married Lieutenant Chevis, whom she had known for five years.

Initially they lived in London, but as Chevis's current posting was at Aldershot they later took a bungalow at nearby Blackdown Camp. Chevis went down to Aldershot on June 6, 1931, and was joined by his wife less than two weeks later. But their stay at Aisne Bungalow, Blackdown, was destined to be tragically short.

Frances Chevis arrived at Blackdown on Friday June 19 and immediately began making plans for what was expected to be a fairly hectic weekend. It would include a visit by friends for cocktails followed by dinner at home on Saturday evening and also an outing to the Aldershot Tattoo. At some time on the Friday, Mrs Chevis telephoned Colbrook's of Aldershot and placed an order for fish and meat – two soles, some beef and two partridges. These items were duly delivered to the bungalow the following day.

At 7.30 on the Saturday evening, their friends had left, Lieutenant and Mrs Chevis sat down to dinner. The meal had been prepared by their cook, Mrs Yeomans, and Chevis's batman, Nicholas Boulger, helped to serve it. He served the peas and potatoes, while Mrs Chevis dealt with the partridges, putting the larger bird on her husbands plate and taking the smaller herself. To this was added sauce and gravy.

It was Lieutenant Chevis who began eating first. But he had probably eaten only a couple of mouthfuls when he complained of a horrible taste. He gave his wife a piece of partridge to taste but she was unable to eat all of it and put it on the side of her plate. Her own partridge also had an unpleasant taste.

"It was the most horrible, bitter taste that I have ever tasted," she recalled later. "It tasted horrible. It burned the back of my throat."

Chevis poured himself a glass of sherry, then another, and his wife also had a glass to try to take the taste away.

"We both tried to eat the vegetables," she said, "but we couldn't eat any more bird, so I rang the bell for the batman and my husband told him to take the bird away and burn it. Cheese and salad were brought in and after coffee had been served, my husband had a sort of spasm. I called a doctor and when my husband had a very bad spell later I gave him some brandy."

Chevis's condition deteriorated rapidly. Gripped by convulsions, he soon lost the use of his legs. He told the doctor that the bird had tasted bitter, like quinine. The doctor had no hesitation in sending both Lieutenant Chevis and his wife to hospital. They were taken to Frimley Cottage Hospital in Surrey, where Mrs Chevis's condition greatly improved under treatment while her husband's worsened further. At midnight his breathing stopped and for the next ten hours, five hospital doctors fought a desperate battle to revive him by means of artificial respiration. It was 9.50 on Sunday morning when they finally admitted defeat and reluctantly announced the death of the 28-year-old officer.

Two days later an inquest was opened at Camberley. The deputy coroner, W.J. Francis, said he understood the partridges had formed part of a consignment that had been dusted with flour before leaving the wholesalers and had been kept in cold storage. Chevis's brother, Captain W.J.C. Chevis, R.E., of Farnborough, gave evidence of identification and said that his brother had been married for only a short time and that he and his wife were very happy. Another witness, Dr Attenborough, said a post-mortem examination had been carried out and some

Right: Mrs Frances Chevis.

Above: Witnesses at the inquest, including Chevis's batman Nicholas Boulger (left), three men from the poultry shop which supplied the partridges and Home Office analyst Dr J.H. Ryffel (right).

ORAY TELEGRAM" IN POISON CASE: DO YOU KNOW THE WRITING?

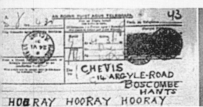

Above: The *Daily Sketch* reproduced the "Hooray" telegram on its front page. Superintendent Stovell is pictured on the right.

of Chevis's organs sent for analysis. He believed that death was due to strychnine poisoning.

The inquest was adjourned until July 21, by which time Frances Chevis was well enough to give evidence. By then the deputy coroner had received the analyst's report, which confirmed that Chevis had died as a result of strychnine poisoning. Mrs Chevis appeared dressed in deep mourning. She confirmed that she and her second husband were very happy and that he had no domestic problems of which she was aware. She spoke of her first marriage, her divorce, and three children of that marriage, and said that she had seen her first husband, Major Jackson, in January, a month after her marriage to Chevis, and again, by accident, earlier in July. Replying to questions from the deputy coroner, she said that the food delivered by Colbrook's had been kept in a meat safe in a wall outside the back door. Asked why she thought her husband had asked his batman to burn the bird, she said he would have been concerned about the possibility of it being given to their dog or cat.

Mrs Chevis was the only witness called. The inquest was again adjourned, this time until August 11.

"I am still making a number of inquiries into this matter because I am very anxious to get to the bottom of it," Mr Francis informed the young widow. "One forms certain theories and it is for the benefit of you and your husband's relatives that I should sift this thing as far as I am able. If you know any circumstances which can possibly help me or the police to get to the bottom of this, I should like you to tell me now or at any time when it comes to your knowledge."

"At the moment there is nothing, I am positive," Mrs Chevis replied.

What the deputy coroner did not say was that he was awaiting the results of police inquiries that were being made, not only in North Hampshire and West Surrey but also in Bournemouth and Dublin. These inquiries included exhaustive checks of the poison registers maintained by chemists shops in the towns surrounding Chevis's home.

At the third and final phase of the inquest on August 11, Frances Chevis was again among the witnesses and this time gave her evidence seated in an armchair, provided after she complained of feeling unwell. She said she had already given the police and the coroner's officer all the information she could. There were no telegrams or correspondence belonging to Lieutenant Chevis which might throw light on the case. Her husband had helped himself to the two glasses of sherry he had drunk to take away the taste of the partridge. Boulger, the batman, would have removed the glasses and Mrs Yeomans, the cook, would have washed them.

"Did your husband leave a will?" asked the deputy coroner.

"Not to my knowledge," said Mrs Chevis.

"Was he insured?"

"Not that I know."

"Where can I get that information?"

"I should say from his bank."

"With regard to your partridge, did you make any complaint?"

"It tasted fusty. There was no bitter or sharp taste."

Mr Francis continued: "Both the partridges were cooked together in a tin and they were basted together in the same fat. It rather amazes me that your partridge should not have tasted of strychnine."

"Yes," said Mrs Chevis. "I should say it was a very musty and unsavoury taste."

"Are you quite sure that your husband told Boulger to burn the partridge?"

"Absolutely."

"You are the only witness who says so. The other witnesses say he told him to destroy it."

"I mean to infer that he said it should be done away with," said Mrs Chevis.

"When one has such bad food, the usual thing is to preserve it and see what is wrong with it. In this case the partridge was burned on his order. There is no question about that. You told me that your husband was very anxious that the dog should not get it?"

"Yes."

The Home Office analyst, Dr J. H. Ryffel, told the inquest that he had examined the contents of the dead man's stomach and also articles from the bungalow, including sink water from the drains, a basin containing dripping, a vegetable dish containing peas and potatoes, an empty tin, a packet of gravy mixture, some anchovy sauce, and a tin of carbolic acid. He had also examined some material from Mrs Chevis after she had been ill. This and material from Lieutenant Chevis, when mixed together, yielded a third of a grain of strychnine. The material from Lieutenant Chevis contained a large amount of strychnine. There was also a small amount of strychnine in the dripping and more in the gravy, which was very bitter. There was no strychnine in the water or the other exhibits.

Dr Ryffel concluded that the total quantity of strychnine associated with the partridges must have amounted to at least two grains. But that, he cautioned, was an extremely rough estimate – the figure would depend on what proportion of the birds had been eaten. He understood that this was only small.

"Then in your view," said the deputy coroner, "if only a small portion of the bird had been eaten, the quantity in the bird was very heavy?"

"It must have been very considerable – more than two grains," replied the analyst. "The minimum fatal dose of strychnine is half-a-grain."

Dr Ryffel said he had tested three other partridges from the cold store of the company from which the suspect birds had been bought and none of them contained strychnine. It was also quite clear that the birds had not picked up strychnine or other poison while alive, since any bird eating strychnine in the quantity consumed by the Chevises would have been dead long before the amount could be absorbed from its crop. On the other hand, if strychnine were injected into it, it would tend to stay there during the cooking.

Police Superintendent Stovell remarked that strychnine could be fatal within two hours but that in this case it was fourteen hours.

"I imagine," said Dr Ryffel, "that in this case the strychnine must have been very slowly absorbed. Actually, Lieutenant Chevis died of failure of respiration. He was kept alive by artificial respiration. Any drug that is used to keep the pulse quiet must also have an effect on respiration, in addition to the convulsions of strychnine poisoning, and it would tend afterwards to make the respiration fail. In this case the long continued convulsions exhausted him, so that he ultimately died of failure of respiration."

Nicholas Boulger, Chevis's batman, asked by Superintendent Stovell on whose authority he had had the bird destroyed, said it was Mrs Chevis who told him to destroy the bird, but not to burn it. He gave it to Mrs Yeomans, the cook, saying, "This is to be destroyed," and she put it in the fire. Afterwards Mrs Chevis came into the kitchen and told him and the cook that the doctor had said her husband was suffering from strychnine poisoning.

"It is a most unfortunate thing," the deputy coroner told the jury, "that both partridges were destroyed, especially the one served to Lieutenant Chevis, and destroyed by his orders. Had the partridge been safely preserved, you might have been able quite easily to have arrived at a definite conclusion, but I doubt very much whether you will be able to do so."

The offending partridges were not only the most crucial material items of evidence in the case but almost the only ones and the fact that they had been destroyed on the instructions of the victim was a peculiar irony. Then there was the odd matter of a mysterious telegram which arrived at the home of Sir William Chevis, the victim's father, in Argyll Road, Boscombe, Bournemouth, at 5 p.m.

on June 24, the day of the young officer's funeral. The telegram read: "Chevis, 14, Argyle-Road, Boscombe, Hants. Hooray, Hooray, Hooray."

"That telegram was unsigned and it was received at the house while Sir William was attending the funeral of his son," said Mr Francis. "Inquiries were at once instituted with a view to tracing the sender, but up to now they have not been successful. The original of the telegram was obtained for inspection and on the back was the signature and address: 'J. Hartigan, Hibernian.' There is an hotel in Dublin called the Royal Hibernian. Inquiries have been made there, and every possible effort has been made to find the sender."

Mr Francis said that whether or not the telegram had any significance, the sending of it was a "very cruel act". He went on: "The Dublin police at once responded to a request to assist in discovering the sender, but in spite of every effort, we have not succeeded in finding who it was. A lot of publicity has been given to this case and a photograph of the telegram has been published."

The telegram had, much to the deputy coroner's displeasure, made the front page of the London newspaper the *Daily Sketch*. Afterwards, a postcard purporting to have been written in London on August 1 was sent to its editor. It read: "Dear Sir, Why do you publish the picture of the 'Hooray' telegram? J. Hartigan."

"I do not know," commented the deputy coroner, "whether or not it is a lunatic at large who is responsible for sending these messages, and I have no evidence concerning this."

Summing up, he told the jury: "There is no doubt that Lieutenant Chevis died from asphyxia following the poisoning caused by eating partridge. What evidence is there here to show whether this was an accident or what it was? You have absolutely no evidence, and I direct you accordingly. There is not a shred of evidence to show how the strychnine came to be on the birds. I sifted all the evidence through before I came here and I could find many little defects, and also that the witnesses did not agree on the points of time and in other respects. But I could find no evidence whatever to lead me or you to any conclusion as to whether this was an accidental death, a foul murder, or whether it was a case of such negligent dealing with things served up for people to eat as amounted to manslaughter."

He added: "There is no evidence at all on which you can find a definite verdict, and that is what I direct you to do. The proper verdict is asphyxia, following strychnine poisoning caused by eating partridge, but insufficient evidence to show how the strychnine came to be in or on the partridge."

After a short consultation among themselves, the jury returned an open verdict, and expressed regret to Lieutenant Chevis's relatives. These relatives then left sadly for their respective homes, still without even a clue to the true circumstances behind the death of Lieutenant Hubert George Chevis of the Royal Artillery. Although it was widely believed that Chevis had been murdered, no one could be certain. And if he was deliberately killed, who was the killer and what was his or her motive? Had he or she also intended to claim the life of Mrs Chevis and if not how could they have been sure to avoid doing so? The police inquiries would continue for some time but the questions were destined to remain unanswered, as they are still unanswered today. The words of one last, mysterious message sent to Sir William Chevis a few days before the final inquest hearing were to prove only too prophetic.

"It is," said the postcard, posted in Belfast on August 4, "a mystery they will never solve. J. Hartigan. Hooray."

7
THE OLD LAG'S ALIBI
The murder of Rose Robinson in 1943

To the drinkers in war-ravaged Portsmouth's city centre, there were few people better known than Rose Robinson, tenant landlady of the John Barleycorn in Commercial Road. She had lived at the beerhouse for thirty-six years and had held the licence for eleven years following the death of her husband. She had witnessed at first-hand the terrible results of German bombing raids on the naval city but, unlike many other properties in Commercial Road, the John Barleycorn had survived the worst of the blitz and Mrs Robinson, despite having a weak heart, had survived with it. But since the bombing began, she had adopted the practice of keeping all her takings in the house, steadily accumulating cash until the end of each month, when she would pay the brewers, Brickwoods. It was common knowledge in Portsmouth that she kept the money in two handbags that went everywhere with her. One bag contained silver and copper coins, the other a wad of £5 and £1 notes held together by elastic bands.

By closing time on the night of Sunday November 28, 1943, Mrs Robinson probably had about £400 in her possession, it being near the end of the month. It was soon after 10 p.m. that evening when the last customer left and Welch, Mrs Robinson's conscientious and scrupulously honest barman, fulfilled his usual duty of locking the doors and windows. Welch was present when the landlady emptied the till and transferred the money to the two bags. He left the premises at 10.35 and heard Mrs Robinson bolt the front door behind him. It was the last time that the licensee of the John Barleycorn was seen alive.

A little under four hours later, a Mrs Louie Smitherman, who lived two doors away, was awakened by a loud banging on the kitchen window at the rear of her house. Then she heard the sound of heavy footsteps – first moving around the kitchen, then, at about 2.30 a.m., outside the house. The footsteps seemed to be moving around the house, from the back along the passageway to the front. For some time, the terrified woman lay silently in her bed in the front ground-floor room, where she regularly slept with her young son because of the threat of bombing. After almost half-an-hour, she mustered enough courage to get out of bed and clamber through the front window to investigate. Between her house and the John Barleycorn she saw a car and four men. Praying that they had not spotted her, she slipped quietly back indoors and into bed. Next morning, she found the back door unbolted and ajar, the kitchen table moved, and the plywood blackout board lying broken outside the kitchen window. But nothing had been stolen.

It was 9 o'clock on that Monday morning when Rose Robinson's cleaning lady, Mrs Firmin, arrived for work at the John Barleycorn as usual. She knocked on the front door but there was no reply, so she went next door to seek help from a young sailor, William Stevens, who was at home on leave. He scaled the garden wall behind the Barleycorn and, finding the back door open, went inside and opened the front door for Mrs Firmin. Then he went upstairs.

Rose Robinson's bedroom was in a state of total disarray. The blackout curtain had been torn from the window and lay near the foot of the bed. The bed itself was in disorder and the dresser had been moved, its drawers ransacked and its contents scattered around the room. Two rugs on the floor were also disarranged and on the bed were the landlady's two handbags and a purse. All three had been emptied.

On a third rug, also disarranged, lay the body, cold and lifeless, of 62-year-old Rose Robinson. Her head and chest were covered by a blue cloth, her dress had been pushed up above her waist. A police surgeon who examined her later concluded that she had been strangled, probably between 2 and 4 o'clock that morning. It was also apparent that, despite her weak heart, Mrs Robinson had fought fiercely in defence of her money and her life. Her injuries included bruises and abrasions as well as the marks of strangulation. These were a deep bruise on the right-hand side of the neck, caused by pressure from a thumb, and three lighter bruises on the left side, apparently caused by fingers. But there were no marks of fingernails, with the possible exception of a thumbnail mark, though even this was not clearly delineated. The eminent pathologist Dr Keith Simpson concluded that the marks had been caused by the grip of a strong right hand belonging to an attacker who was either sitting astride or kneeling beside the struggling woman at the time. He proposed a scenario that had Mrs Robinson rushing from her bed towards the window to call for help, falling to her knees, hitting her head on the window-sill, grabbing the blackout curtain, and being dragged away and strangled by her assailant, perhaps as a by-product of an attempt to silence her.

Police began making door-to-door inquiries in the area and soon learned of Mrs Smitherman's experience. It did not take them long to conclude that the intruder or intruders had entered her house after mistaking it for the John Barleycorn, moving on to their intended target after realizing their error. Other inquiries led police to issue descriptions of a sailor and a young woman who had been seen near the beerhouse on the night in question. A week later, on December 7, a 22-year-old seaman and a 21-year-old blonde-haired woman appeared in court in connection with the alleged theft of a banjo and a coat and, in the case of the man, who had a long list of previous convictions, of being absent from the Royal Navy. There was some excitement when the Chief Constable of Portsmouth, Mr A.C. West, applied for a remand in custody so that the couple could be questioned about "circumstances of an extremely important nature". The remand was granted, but when the couple returned to court on December 14, there was no mention of the "extremely important circumstances". No evidence was offered against the young woman, who was discharged; the seaman was sentenced to six months' hard labour for the offences mentioned at the earlier hearing.

Suspicions that the young couple were in some way connected with the killing of Rose Robinson had proved unfounded and the detectives working on the case were back almost where they started. The only other clue they had, if indeed it was a clue, was a small black button with thread attached, which had been found on the frame of the broken kitchen window used to gain entry to the John Barleycorn. But finding a button was one thing; matching it to the coat sleeve from which it came was quite another. Inquiries were as extensive as they could be amid the chaos and confusion of wartime and everyone in the area with known criminal connections was questioned. But the trail was cold and the police resigned themselves to the likelihood that the murder was destined to remain unsolved.

Then came a totally unexpected development. On the afternoon of December 21, 1943, constables Herbert Baker and Angus McLean of the Metropolitan Police were on plain-clothes duty in Waterloo Road, London, when they saw a man walk into the Anchor Cafe with a pair of shoes under one arm. The shoes looked new, the man looked rather scruffy and the officers were specifically looking out for people dealing in stolen property, so they followed. The man handed one of the shoes to the woman behind the counter.

"Know anyone who wants a pair of shoes for twenty-five bob?" he asked, unaware that there were two policemen standing behind him.

The woman handed the shoe to the officer.

"My brother sent them to me for Christmas," the man blustered. "They're too big for me, and if you're not satisfied, I'll go with you to the station."

According to the police version of events, details of which the man was later to dispute, he was subsequently told he was being arrested for unlawful possession of the shoes, at which he suddenly announced: "I'm wanted for things far more serious than this. The Yard wants me. It's the trapdoor for me now. I'm glad you picked me up. It'll do you good."

On his way by van to Kennington Road police station, the man, Harold Loughans, produced a silver cigarette box and gave it to PC McLean, telling him: "There's a Christmas box for you. I know this will be my last Christmas." Arriving at the station, he became distressed and started to cry. According to the police, he continued: "I'm glad I'm in. I've been through hell for the past three weeks. I've been a bastard all my life and I'll finish as I lived. I was sorry for it the moment I'd done it. I haven't slept since. It preyed on my mind. She must have had a weak heart, poor old girl!"

As the police listened interestedly, Loughans rambled on about the murder and other crimes he said he had committed. At times he became emotional as he told them: "I've done a dozen jobs and I tied a woman to a bed last week at St Albans; hit her on the head with a torch and robbed her. Got a cigarette case and other things from there. I've done jobs at Mill Hill, Edgware and other places I can't remember. I know this is the end of the road for me. I want to say I done a murder job in Hampshire about fourteen days ago."

Later he continued: "It's a relief to get it off my mind. I had to stop her screaming, but I didn't mean to kill the old girl, but you know what it is when a woman screams. You were just too late – the woman was outside with the case. I told her if ever she saw me with any men looking like cops to get away. All the jobs I have been doing have been worrying me, and since I did the big job at

Portsmouth, where I got the money and when I strangled the old woman at the beerhouse, to get it off my mind I have been doing jobs every day. The money is with a woman friend of mine in a suitcase. I have spent about £50 and I gave her £200."

Invited to make a formal statement, Loughans unhesitatingly agreed and proceeded to dictate the details and sign the document.

"About the end of November 1943," said the statement, "I went to Portsmouth and while I was there I went into the Fox-and-something-else public house for a drink. I think it was dinner time. The day before that I was at Portsmouth as well. I got talking to one of the customers, and he told me that the old lady of the pub had about £2,000 in the house. I thought it over and later that day, after the pub closed, I went to the back of the pub and climbed over a gate or wall and got in, so far as I can remember, through a window. When I got in and I was looking through a room when the woman, I should think she was about sixty years, came in. I grabbed her and told her to keep quiet. She screamed, and I just put my hands round her throat. She became quiet, and I thought she had fainted and I left her lying on the floor and I found a lot of money. They were mostly £5 notes tied up, I think, with string. I opened some cupboards and drawers and I think I got the money out of a little desk. I also got a lot of loose cash out of a till drawer downstairs. I shall have to think a bit. I didn't intend killing her – I only thought I would stop her screaming. When I did that job I hired a car in London and came back from Portsmouth by the same car."

The Metropolitan officers would probably not have realized it, for they would not have had detailed knowledge of the case, but the statement varied in several respects from the true facts of the murder at the John Barleycorn. It stated that the pub was called the Fox and something, that the woman interrupted the intruder by coming into a room, that she was strangled with two hands rather than one, that there was cash in the till downstairs, that the notes were tied with string rather than elastic bands, that the money was in a little desk. The statement also made no mention of a break-in carried out by mistake at a neighbouring house. Nevertheless, people do not confess to unsolved murders every day and there was enough in the statement to justify a telephone call to the Portsmouth City Constabulary.

Detective Inspector Lamport and Detective Sergeant Atkins reached Kennington in the early hours of December 22 and began interviewing Loughans at 2 a.m. He told them that the statement he had already made was correct and then gave them a further summary of the events it described. Interestingly, this oral account, as recalled by the two officers at a later date, corresponded much more closely with the evidence found in the John Barleycorn. According to Lamport and Atkins, who were, of course, familiar with the case, Loughans told them: "When I got upstairs in the public house, I saw a woman in the back room, and as she screamed I grabbed her by the throat and she fell down by the window, and as she fell the black-out fell down. I held her on the floor and I thought she had fainted. She looked awful, so I covered her face with a piece of cloth I took off the bed. Did the old lady have a weak heart? I cannot understand it, as she went quiet right away. I know I took a lot of money out of some bags on the dressing table and got out of the pub."

Loughans was taken to Portsmouth by car and slept most of the way. But, according to the police, he awoke as they approached the city and as they came within fifty yards of the John Barleycorn, he looked out of the window and said: "This is somewhere near the place."

He was taken to Fratton Police Station, where he dictated a further statement to the Portsmouth officers and signed it. Once again it differed in several respects from his original statement and accorded very closely with the facts known to the police.

"I cannot remember the name of the public house," it said. "I think it was the Fox. It was in Commercial Road. I cannot be sure of the date I broke in, but I think it was the 28th November. When I climbed over the wall at the back of the public house, I had a look round the garden. I then went to the window at the back of another house and got in through a window into a bar. I went upstairs and went into several rooms. In the back room I saw a woman. There was no light in the room and I flashed my torch on to her. She must have heard me and got out of bed, as she was wearing some clothes. She asked me who I was. I did not answer her, and she started to scream. I went for her and grabbed her by the throat with my right hand. She fell down near a window and as she fell the blackout fell down from the window. I held her down on the floor and then I thought she had fainted. She looked very queer, and I covered her face with a piece of cloth I found in the room. There were two large handbags on a dressing table with a glass top. Those bags were full of money. When she screamed she rushed towards the bags and tried to grab them. I tipped the money out of the bags into my overcoat. There was a lot of silver and £5 notes and £1 notes. I noticed that the old lady was not wearing any rings. I did not take her jewellery. I unbolted the back door and went into the yard and then into an empty house next door, through this house and into the street. I jumped into a motor car which was waiting for me and went away. I do not want to say anything about the car or who was driving it."

The statement continued: "I left Portsmouth and went straight back to London. I did not count the money, but I think I had about £450 in notes and about £20 in silver. About £300 of this sum was in £5 notes. When I got back to London I gave £50 to a young lady and the rest of the money I kept in a suitcase. I remember when I left the public house there was a woman came out of a house near the pub. I heard accidentally that the old lady died in Portsmouth and since this time I have been unable to sleep and have been drinking heavily. I cannot remember everything very clearly, but I did not mean to kill the old lady and I am very sorry. I told the young lady who I was with that if ever I was arrested she was to take the suitcase and money and go away. She saw me arrested in London on the 21st December and I gave her the tip to go. I do not wish to give any information about the young lady or the man who drove the car."

Harold Loughans, aged 47, described as a married man and a labourer, of no fixed abode, appeared before Portsmouth magistrates within a few hours of his arrival in the city. He was charged with feloniously, wilfully and with malice aforethought killing and murdering Rose Ada Robinson between 10.30 p.m. on November 28 and 9 a.m. on November 29. The Chief Constable applied for a remand in custody for fourteen days, which was granted. Loughans declined to apply for legal aid but stated that he would like to be tried at the first available opportunity.

"He sat in court and had occasional snatches of conversation with his police escort while a number of small cases were dealt with," Portsmouth's *Evening News* reported. "When his name was called he walked into the dock and stood with head bowed. He was wearing a light fawn-coloured overcoat over a dark suit. He had no collar and tie."

Loughans' overcoat was to play an important part in the case. Police later claimed that when they took the coat from him on December 22, he told them: "It's all right, Inspector. You won't find any buttons there. After I did the job, I found I had a button missing. I got the wind up and when I got back to London I pulled them all off." It was, however, a statement that, like many elements of the other oral and written statements attributed to him, Loughans was later to deny.

Following his first court appearance, police began to make extensive inquiries into Loughans' background and they soon learned that he was an old lag with a significant number of criminal convictions against his name. He was disabled from an accident at some time in the past, which had severed the fingers of his right hand at the second knuckles. His latest prison sentence had ended as recently as October 15, after which he worked at a mill near Halifax in Yorkshire. He left Huddersfield by train late on the evening of November 27, being seen off by a Methodist minister, and arrived in London at 5.15 the following morning. At 10.30 he told someone of his intention to try for a job at the Royal Hospital, Chelsea, next morning. Then he visited the Methodist centre at Westminster Central Hall and spoke to Sister Lillie Sweet, telling her he had just served a twenty-year sentence for murdering his best friend. Sister Sweet, a Methodist deaconess, gave him five shillings for food and the conversation made such an impression on her that she made a note in her diary: "Harold Loughans – Murder." The following day, November 29, Loughans called at the Royal Hospital, Chelsea, as he had said he would, and was hired as a porter. He remained in the job for only two days before walking out with the suit of clothes the hospital had given him.

Although Loughans' presence in Yorkshire on November 27 did not concur with his first statement, which declared that he was in Portsmouth that day, his known movements on the following two days appeared to allow ample time for him to travel from London to Portsmouth on November 28, carry out the crime at the beerhouse and return to London overnight. Other evidence linking him to the crime was also beginning to accumulate. He had, of course, confessed repeatedly to the murder and had signed two statements to that effect. But there were also some interesting discoveries at the Metropolitan police laboratory. Staff there had examined his coat, trousers and boots and various items from Rose Robinson's bedroom. In the welt of the left boot, they found a fibre of green wool similar to the fibres of a mat near the bedroom door, and also a piece of hemp similar to the undyed fibre of the bedside mat. The turn-up of the left trouserleg contained two fibres similar to those of a third mat. On the right sleeve of Loughans' coat was a feather that resembled the feathers in the eiderdown and inside the tuck of the left cuff was a knot of thread similar to the thread on the small black button found on the window frame. Two of the larger buttons down the front of the coat were looser than the rest and had been sewn on with thread of the same type.

Harold Loughans made a second court appearance fourteen days after the first but again had little to say and declined legal aid. But on January 6, 1944, his attitude suddenly changed. He requested a meeting with his prison governor and told him that he was innocent and that the police had put details of the murder into his mouth as he made his "confessions". He added that he was connected to the crime "in a way" and had received some of the victim's money and that this was why he had not declared his innocence before. But even now he was not prepared to disclose any other facts, stating that he wanted to "sweeten the police", who were likely to charge him with theft and assault if the murder case fell through.

At his third court appearance on January 12, Loughans stood in the dock and declared: "This murder charge I am not guilty of." But of the nature of his defence, he gave not the slightest clue, and the prosecution still had no inkling of it when they arrived for the trial at the Hampshire Assizes in Winchester at the beginning of March. Exactly how Loughans intended to keep his head from the beckoning noose was a mystery to all but him and his legal advisers. These included his counsel, John Maude, K.C., and Guy Willett, and their well-known instructing solicitor from Southampton, a Mr Hiscock, while Joshua D. Casswell, K.C., and John Platts-Mills appeared for the Director of Public Prosecutions.

As the barristers prepared in the robing room a few minutes before the trial was due to begin, John Maude said to Casswell: "I may as well tell you that I'm not going to rely on Loughans' evidence in this case. I'm going to call some completely independent witnesses who will provide him with an alibi."

"Do you mean to say you're going to try to prove Loughans wasn't even in Portsmouth on the night of the murder?" asked the surprised prosecution counsel.

"That's right, Josh!" grinned Maude.

The trial opened before Mr Justice Atkinson and a jury of nine men and three women. Asked whether he was guilty or not guilty, Loughans replied in a clear voice: "I am not guilty, sir."

An important witness for the prosecution was Dr Keith Simpson, the pathologist. He told the court that Rose Robinson would have been capable of "vigorous self-protective action" but that the advanced senile condition of her heart would have given her less reserve than a woman in perfect health. She had been strangled and her injuries were in keeping with her having been gripped from the front by a right hand with very considerable strength and with the grip maintained. From plaster casts of Loughans' malformed right hand, he had formed the view that he would have been capable of causing the right-handed grip upon the neck.

A surprise revelation during the prosecution evidence came from Detective

Inspector Lamport, of Portsmouth CID. Cross-examined by Mr Maude, he told the court that in 1941, or a little earlier, Harold Loughans had confessed to the Staffordshire police to a murder in Scotland. It turned out to be a bogus confession.

In his opening remarks for the defence, Maude told the jury: "We know that there are persons, not necessarily insane, who will from time to time confess to crimes they have not committed. This man is such a person. Sometimes it is done to annoy, and you will find in the accused a raw bit of life. This is a man who has spent years in prison. By the time you have spent year after year in prison, there comes a time when life does not seem to be very attractive."

Even at this stage of the hearing, the prosecution had only a vague idea of what was to come. John Maude had no reason to keep them waiting any longer.

"On the night of the murder," he told the jury, "my client was in Warren Street Underground station in London. You are going to see witnesses who were in that station. There are three women who, when interviewed, were able to remember this man quite distinctly. Remembering Loughans would not be difficult. He has a distinctive face and a hand nobody would forget."

Maude said that three married women and a man would testify that they had seen Loughans in the Underground station, which was being used at night as an air-raid shelter, on the night in question. But before they gave evidence, Harold Loughans himself was called to the stand. Standing with his hands in his pockets, apparently unmoved by the gravity of his position, he spent almost four hours in the witness box, telling the court of his prison sentences in the past and of his bogus confession to a murder in Scotland, which he had made to give police "a little bit of trouble to go on with" after they had "knocked me off for loitering".

"Why did you tell the police in this case that you had murdered Mrs Robinson?" asked the defence counsel.

Loughans said it went back to his job at a mill in Yorkshire, which he started after his release from prison in October 1943. He claimed that the police had harassed him. "Every time I left this job to go home to have a meal, the police were there, in the vicinity of the bus stop," he said. "They were there every night to see me off the neighbourhood. I got fed up and I was not in a position to retaliate or anything. They had the upper hand of me all the time."

Loughans told how he left Huddersfield for London late on November 27 and, because he was out of prison on licence, reported to Scotland Yard at 10 o'clock the following morning. He then went to the Methodist centre at Westminster and later to Watford police station to see if he could get in touch with a probation officer. That evening he took an Underground train from Watford to Warren Street thinking he would be able to get shelter in the Underground. He arrived at about 8.15 or 8.30 and, after a short stroll as far as Tottenham Court Road, stayed at Warren Street until 5.15 the next morning.

"This was a complete surprise to the prosecution," Josh Casswell recalls in his memoirs. "This was the first we knew, other than earlier that day during Maude's opening speech for the defence, that Loughans was going to contend that at the time Mrs Robinson met her death he was in a London Underground shelter over eighty miles away."

Loughans told the court that his confession to the murder was a "hoax and a grand joke" until it came to court, when it got serious and he was advised to change his attitude. His original knowledge of the Portsmouth murder came from a cutting from the *News of the World*. On arrival at Portsmouth following his arrest, he was woken by the police and, as the car slowed down, was asked to look out of the window. His attention was drawn to the John Barleycorn and he was told that that was where the murder was committed.

"Where did you get the majority of the facts in your statements?" asked John Maude.

"They were given to me by the police by asking questions and giving me the answers at the same time," Loughans replied.

"He said," recalls Casswell, "that he had nothing to do with the murder, or with the planning of the robbery, and explained away all the facts set out in his alleged confessions as having been suggested to him by the police from their own knowledge of what had been found at the scene of the tragedy."

In cross-examination, Casswell and Platts-Mills tried to show that this was unlikely, as the officers to whom Loughans first confessed belonged to the Metropolitan Police and would not have been well-informed about a Portsmouth case. But, as John Maude was later to point out to the jury, that first statement contained a number of factual errors, whereas the later ones made with the help of Portsmouth detectives who were fully conversant with the case tied in very well with the finer points of the evidence found at the John Barleycorn. Did not this support Loughans' contention that the police put details of the murder into his mouth?

The support for Loughans' alibi was stronger than the prosecution could possibly have feared. The defence called four witnesses who clearly remembered seeing him at Warren Street Underground station on the night of November 28-29. They included James Rycroft, a rail relayer with the London Passenger

Transport Board, who saw Loughans talking to three women, all of whom he knew. He had particularly noticed that the man had four fingers missing on his right hand. But how could he be sure that it was a Sunday night? Because Sunday night was the quietest night of the week and the only time they did any relaying or track repairs, he replied.

The prosecution were, as Casswell admits, "somewhat shattered by this impressive evidence". They clung to the hope that it was not conclusive, that perhaps Rycroft had got the date wrong.

"But not at all," says Casswell. "Rycroft was followed into the witness box by William Bull, a ganger also in the employment of the L.P.T.B. He brought with him a 'record of works' book which showed beyond doubt that the only night in November when Rycroft had been at work at Warren Street Station was that night, November 28-29."

Edith Costors, aged 25, also remembered seeing Loughans in the tube station that night. She did not know his name, and had not seen him before or since, until the trial, but they had talked about her baby and he had even offered to hold it when it cried. She remembered that he had "a finger" missing from his right hand, that he had said he came from Huddersfield, that they talked until 12.20 a.m., that he slept two bunks away from her, that she had covered his feet with his raincoat at 3 a.m. and that she woke him at 5.45.

Edith Hatcher and Rachael Pickering were also at Warren Street that night. Mrs Hatcher lent Loughans a pillow, Mrs Pickering remembered him saying that he had just come from Huddersfield that day.

"I noticed his hand and turned my head away," she said.

Casswell swallowed hard.

"Clearly," recalls the leading counsel for the defence, "if the jury believed this evidence, or even if they were merely doubtful whether it was true or not, it was their duty to acquit, for if they were left in doubt, the prosecution had failed to satisfy them beyond reasonable doubt of the guilt of the accused. I was not at all sanguine about the outcome: after all, no man can be in two places at once."

Surprisingly, perhaps, the twelve men and women of the jury found it impossible to agree on a verdict. Two weeks later, on March 27, 1944, the Harold Loughans circus reassembled at the Old Bailey for a retrial in the Central Criminal Court. Most of the personnel were the same but there was a different jury, of course, and a different judge – Mr Justice Cassels. There was also soon to be one last surprise from a defence team who seemed to have an endless supply of white rabbits hidden up their sleeves.

LABOURER ACCUSED OF

MARRIED MAN BEFORE CITY MAGISTRATES

Brought From London

A MAN was detained in London last night in connexion with the murder of Mrs. Rose Ada Robinson, the 63-year-old licensee of the John Barleycorn beerhouse, Commercial Road, Portsmouth, who was found dead in her bedroom on the morning of November 29.

He is Harold Joughans (47), a married man, described as a labourer, of no fixed abode.

He was brought to Portsmouth early this morning and was charged with the murder of Mrs. Robinson, at the Magistrates' Court before Mr. L. R. Maidment and Mr. T. Henly.

He sat in court and had occasional snatches of conversation with his police escort while a number of small cases were dealt with.

When his name was called he walked into the dock and stood with head bowed.

He was wearing a light fawn coloured overcoat over a dark suit. He had no collar and tie.

CLERK'S QUESTION

The Magistrate's Clerk (Mr. B. J. Tay) asked him if Harold was his only Christian name, and he replied that it was.

He was then charged with feloniously, wilfully, and with malice aforethought killing and murdering Rose Ada Robinson between 10.30 p.m. on Nov. 28, and 9 a.m. on Nov. 29.

Detective-Inspector J. Lamport said that at 9.45 a.m. on Nov. 29, in company with Detective Supt. Fuggle, he went to 518, Commercial Road, Landport, where he saw the body of Mrs. Robinson lying in an upstairs bedroom.

FOUND STRANGLED

On Nov. 30 a post-mortem examination was made by Dr.

Keith Simpson, and death was found to be due to strangulation.

Extensive inquiries, said the Inspector, had been made by the Criminal Investigation Department, and as a result of certain information received, he went with Det.-Sgt. Atkins to Kennington Lane police station, where at 2 o'clock that morning he saw the prisoner.

The prisoner was conveyed to Portsmouth, where he was cautioned and charged. He replied: "Yes."

REMAND FOR FORTNIGHT

The Chief Constable (Mr. A. C. West) said that in view of the many inquiries which have to be made before the facts could be presented to the Director of Public Prosecutions, he asked for a remand for 14 days in custody.

When asked by the Chairman if he had anything to say, Joughans replied, "No, I do not wish for anything."

Mr. Maidment: Perhaps you had better not say anything now.

PRISONER'S REQUEST

"I would like to say this," broke in the prisoner, "If it is possible will you send me to the first place possible for trial?"

The Chairman asked what the prisoner had said, and the Magistrates' Clerk said that

he wished to go to the first possible place for trial, as he wished to get it over.

The Chairman: We cannot deal with that until the remand has expired.

LEGAL AID REJECTED

The Chairman asked Joughans if he wanted legal aid, and the prisoner in a quiet, slightly husky voice said, "No, I don't want anything."

Are you sure about that? Would you like to have assistance?

The prisoner again answered "No, sir."

The Magistrates' Clerk told him that if he thought the matter over during the time he was on remand he could make application, but he could name someone to look after his interests now.

The Chairman: Very well, if you are so later on, you can have legal aid. You will be remanded in custody for 14 days.

The John Barleycorn beerhouse at Mile End.

Right: Portsmouth's *Evening News* breaks the story of the arrest of Harold Loughans (mis-spelt "Joughans"). *(Picture by courtesy of The News, Portsmouth)*

Below: The public bar at the John Barleycorn beerhouse. *(Picture by courtesy of Hampshire Chief Constable)*

In its early and middle stages, the trial unfolded much as before. The same prosecution witnesses were called, the same questions asked and much the same answers given. Loughans recounted his version of events and his alibi witnesses followed him to the stand. Then it was time for John Maude to pull the latest trump card from his increasingly impressive hand.

"I call my next witness – Sir Bernard Spilsbury," he said.

Not for the first time in the John Barleycorn saga, a ripple of alarm spread through the prosecution ranks.

"This eminent pathologist – perhaps the most renowned of all time – had never yet been mentioned in connection with this case," Casswell recalls. "In what possible way could his evidence assist the defence and what could he say that had not been given in evidence at the first trial?"

The answer was soon made clear as Sir Bernard stepped self-assuredly into the box and announced that he had examined Loughans' right hand and arm and was sure the man could not possibly have strangled Rose Robinson. It was obvious, he said, because the accident that had deprived him of the four fingers of his right hand had also removed the muscles of the arm. It happened some years before, he added, when Loughans caught his hand in some machinery. As he wrenched it free, his arm muscles were pulled away, and although parts of his fingers were saved, they could be bent in any direction and were so useless that in Spilsbury's opinion they were incapable even of leaving a scratch.

"When Maude sat down," says Casswell, "and I rose to cross-examine, I wondered what on earth I could possibly do with such testimony and from such a distinguished source."

He tried to persuade Sir Bernard that his judgement might be in error. But the pathologist was not for turning.

"Once Spilsbury had made up his mind, it was almost impossible to shift him. He had already given the jury his considered view, and that was all there was to it. However, I obtained an admission that Spilsbury did not know that the injury to Loughans' hand and arm had taken place as long ago as over thirty years before. He also conceded that over such a long period the accused must have acquired a great deal of practice in the use of the mutilated limb. But that was all. Further than that, Spilsbury would not qualify his finding one iota."

To worsen matters further for the Crown, their own counterpart to Spilsbury, Keith Simpson, had given a less than perfect performance in the witness box. He had not even examined the prisoner's hand personally, relying instead on a plaster cast and photographs. And he had uttered manifest rubbish. "The shortened

Sir Bernard Spilsbury.

fingers would increase the strength of the grip," he had pontificated. "The shorter the finger, the stronger the power created at the end."

If the alibi evidence was not enough to seal the case in Loughans' favour, then Spilsbury's evidence was. His opinion was crucial, if not decisive, and it took the jury little more than an hour to decide that the prisoner was not guilty of murdering Rose Ada Robinson. It was not a verdict with which, in the circumstances, any fair-minded person could disagree.

But if Harold Loughans was innocent, and he clearly was, then how did he come to know so much about the crime committed at the Commercial Road beerhouse on the night of November 28-29, 1943? How did he come to have fibres in his clothing that matched fibres from Rose Robinson's room? Was it coincidence that the thread on the button found on the window frame resembled the button thread found on his coat?

If Harold Loughans was innocent, then who did rob and murder the landlady of the John Barleycorn?

The questions were of only passing interest to a public preoccupied with the task of seeing off Adolf Hitler. They were of even less interest to the man who had almost talked his way to the scaffold and then had to talk his way back again. Life behind bars held few terrors for him and he quickly resumed his old criminal habits. Within two months of his release, he was back inside, serving a five-year sentence for housebreaking.

8
DEATH ON THE DURBAN CASTLE
The murder of Gay Gibson in 1947

Amid the docklands bustle of postwar Southampton, the arrival of the Union Castle liner *Durban Castle* would normally have been a routine matter likely to pass unnoticed by the vast majority of the town's inhabitants. But this was not the case on October 25, 1947, as the vessel steamed into the Solent on the last leg of her regular voyage from Cape Town. On the dockside, a gaggle of reporters gathered to await the ship's arrival, while two officers of the Southampton Constabulary waited to board a launch which would take them to a rendezvous with the ship in Cowes Roads. On the strength of a radio message received at the shipping lines office in London, not only Southampton but the whole of Britain was abuzz over news that of fifty-seven first class passengers who left Cape Town on October 10, only fifty-six were still on board. The fifty-seventh was reported to have disappeared through a cabin porthole seven days into the voyage.

The missing passenger was Eileen Isabella Ronnie Gibson, a beautiful young actress who had adopted the stage name Gay Gibson. Born in India of white English parents in 1926, she spent much of her early life abroad but, like many children in her position, was sent to England for her education. From an early age she dreamed of a stage career, and while serving in the forces after World War II, she succeeded in getting a transfer to Stars in Battledress, a theatrical company of service personnel, with whom she toured England, Wales, France and Germany. She left the services in February 1947 and went to South Africa, where her father was working near Durban. A fortnight later she moved to Johannesburg, where she landed a part in a play called *The Silver Cord*. Her success in this led to parts in several radio shows for the South African Broadcasting Company and these, in turn, to a leading role in a major stage production of Clifford Odets' play *Golden Boy*. The show was an instant success, attracting glowing reviews from the critics, but its run was abruptly halted after only eleven days due to the theatre's enforced closure as a fire hazard. Plans were made to move the production from Johannesburg to Pretoria but Gay Gibson suddenly and unexpectedly announced that she would not be staying in the cast and would instead be taking the next available boat to England. She told the producer, Henry Gilbert, that her "boyfriend" was paying her passage.

As the *Durban Castle* headed away from Cape Town on October 10, Gay Gibson soon discovered that most of the other first-class passengers were elderly or middle-aged and unlikely to offer ideal companionship for the 21-year-old actress during the long voyage to Southampton. As the journey progressed, Gay took little interest in the ship's social activities. She kept herself to herself and spent much of her time alone on deck, leaning over the rail and gazing out to sea. A cabin stewardess, Eileen Field, later recalled that she seemed cheerful enough, but some of her fellow passengers thought she appeared listless and in low spirits.

The person who probably paid most attention to Gay Gibson during the early days of the voyage was James Camb, a 30-year-old deck steward in the first class section of the ship. Although he claimed to love deeply his wife and three-year-old daughter back home in Glasgow, getting to know women passengers had become something of a speciality for Camb during his fourteen years as a merchant seaman. He was a good looking young man, rather thick set, with dark hair, bright eyes and a clear complexion, and he was always smartly turned out in his black and white steward's uniform. For him, a certain class of unattached female passenger was easy prey, and indulging in these affairs of the ocean wave became an habitual pastime for him over the years.

"I had always looked upon these sea-voyage romances as part of the game of being a steward aboard a luxury liner," he admitted in a newspaper article many years later.

According to his own account, Camb's first meeting with Gay Gibson occurred on the second day out of Cape Town. She was sitting alone in the Long

Gallery at the time and she called him over to ask for a drink. She was very talkative, he said, and they chatted for fifteen minutes. She told him about her developing acting career and about her recent work in Johannesburg. She also told him she was "crazy" about a man called Charles, whom she had been going around with in the South African city.

"She said she was very fond of this man but that possible complications might have set in," Camb recalled. "I said: 'You don't mean to tell me you're going to have a baby?' She said it was rather too soon yet to know. I said: 'If that is the position, why don't you marry the man?' She said it was not quite as easy as that, as he was already married."

Exactly how the relationship between Camb and Gay Gibson developed over the next few days is not entirely clear. Other passengers on the *Durban Castle* noticed nothing unusual between them, but there was a special arrangement by which Camb prepared a tea tray for Gay each afternoon and a supper tray each evening. Late at night he would also leave a glass of rum outside the bar for her to collect. They were certainly on friendly terms.

On the evening of October 17, Camb was heard to tell Gay Gibson: "I have a bone to pick with you, and a big one at that!" That same evening Gay dined with her two usual table companions, a Mr Hopwood and a Wing Commander Bray, and after taking part in three or four dances, she left them at 11 p.m. and returned to her cabin, number 126. She emerged some time later and went to the smokeroom on the promenade deck, where she remained until 12.40 a.m. At that time she was escorted to her cabin by Mr Hopwood, but she did not stay there long, and at 1 a.m. the boatswain's mate saw her standing by the deck rails, clothed in her black evening gown and smoking a cigarette. It was the last time anyone other than James Camb saw Gay Gibson, alive or dead.

Just before 3 a.m., however, two nightwatchmen, Murray and Steer, were dozing in a galley on A deck when they heard a bell ringing on B deck. Steer went to investigate and found that both the red and the green lights outside Cabin 126 were on, indicating that the buttons requesting a steward and a stewardess had both been pressed. The lights inside the cabin were on and he knocked and tried the door, which was not bolted. He pushed it open slightly, but it was immediately slammed in his face, though not before he had seen a man's face and right hand. As the door closed, he heard the man say, "It's all right."

Steer went back to Murray, the senior nightwatchman, and both then went to the cabin. This time the door was locked or bolted and they could hear nothing. For several minutes they stood indecisively outside, then Murray went

Gay Gibson.

off to report to the officer on the bridge, telling him that there was a man in Miss Gibson's cabin. He implied that the man in question was a passenger. The officer commented that it was not their business to interfere with passengers' morals and no further action was taken. According to Murray, he returned to B deck to find that Steer had gone and the cabin was now in darkness; Steer's version was that the light was out before Murray's first arrival and that he did not leave the cabin door until Murray returned from the bridge.

Four hours later, at 7.30, Miss Field, the cabin stewardess, knocked on the door of Cabin 126. There was no reply. After a few seconds she knocked again and turned the door knob. To her surprise, for Gay Gibson usually kept the door bolted, it was unlocked. But before entering, Miss Field called out: "Miss Gibson? Miss Gibson?" Still there was no reply.

On entering the cabin, Miss Field noticed that the porthole was wide open and sunlight from a clear blue sky was streaming on to a somewhat disarranged bed. The bedclothes were pulled down to the foot of the bed and there were slight stains on the pillows and sheets. The passenger's black evening dress was hanging in its usual place but her black pyjamas and yellow dressing gown were missing. Remembering a recent conversation with James Camb, in which he had told her that Miss Gibson thought she might be two or three months pregnant, Miss Field began to feel increasingly concerned for the passenger's welfare. She wondered if Miss Gibson had gone to the bathroom, but a check with the bedroom steward revealed that this was not the case. After returning briefly to the deserted cabin, Miss Field went straight to her superior to report that the actress was missing.

By the time the ship's captain, Arthur Patey, became aware of Miss Gibson's disappearance, it was 10 a.m. and seven hours had elapsed since Steer had made his vain attempt to enter Cabin 126. Captain Patey immediately gave orders for the ship to be searched; he also broadcast an appeal for information to everyone on board. Both were unsuccessful and at 10.20 the captain had the ship's course reversed and extended his appeal to other shipping, asking them to keep a lookout. For an hour or so, the *Durban Castle* retraced its course but by 11.40 Captain Patey had concluded that any further searching of the shark-infested waters was pointless and the voyage to Southampton was resumed.

By this time rumour and speculation were rife among both passengers and crew. Some remembered Gay Gibson's apparently depressed state of mind and suicide was widely considered a possibility. But Captain Patey, having learned of the state in which the missing passenger's cabin was found, was not satisfied and began questioning other members of the crew. Among them were the night-watchmen Steer and Murray, and Steer rather hesitantly revealed that the man he saw for a fleeting moment when answering the call to Cabin 126 was the steward James Camb. Camb himself, unaware of this revelation, told Captain Patey that he had turned in at 12.45 and had not been near Miss Gibson's or any other passenger's cabin after that. Another steward, William Pott, who shared a cabin with Camb, said that he too had slept from 12.45 until 6 a.m., when he awoke to see Camb asleep in his bunk. But he also stated that later in the morning he had seen Camb going about his routine cleaning-up work wearing his steward's long-sleeved jacket – an odd choice of garment in the heat of the tropics, where stewards normally wore just a singlet and trousers in the early part of the day.

Captain Patey decided to have Camb medically examined. The steward asked him why.

"You're suspected of having played some part in Miss Gibson's disappearance, and it's in your own interest that you be examined," said Captain Patey.

Camb thanked him for the explanation, consented to the medical examin-ation, and turned to go. But as he left, he muttered, almost to himself: "Why all this suspicion? Let's get down to rock bottom."

The examination was carried out at noon the following day by the ship's surgeon. He found three groups of injuries on Camb's body – scratches and abrasions on the lower right of his neck, more scratches on the left collar-bone, and yet more scratches on the right wrist. Camb explained them away by saying that he had used and that he had scratched himself in bed to relieve severe itching two days earlier. But the surgeon could find no evidence of any skin complaint likely to cause such itching. He also considered that the scratch marks were consistent with having been caused by fingernails in the early hours of October 18.

Later that day, James Camb wrote two reports to Captain Patey. One gave an account of his movements on the night of Gay Gibson's disappearance and reaffirmed his claim that he did not go near her cabin. The other repeated the explanations for his injuries that he had given to the ship's surgeon. But Captain Patey had already radioed a summary of the circumstances to his head office in London and received his orders: "Padlock and seal cabin. Disturb nothing. CID officers will come aboard at Cowes Road."

The instructions were followed and the passengers and crew carried on as normally as they could, although a fairly close watch was kept on Camb. Two

Above: F.D. Steer, one of the Durban Castle's nightwatchmen. *(Photo: Southern Daily Echo)*

Right: Durban Castle stewardess Eileen Field. *(Photo: Southern Daily Echo)*

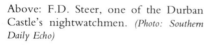

Above: The corridor leading to Cabin 126.

Below: Gay Gibson's cabin showing the bell-buttons (left) and porthole.

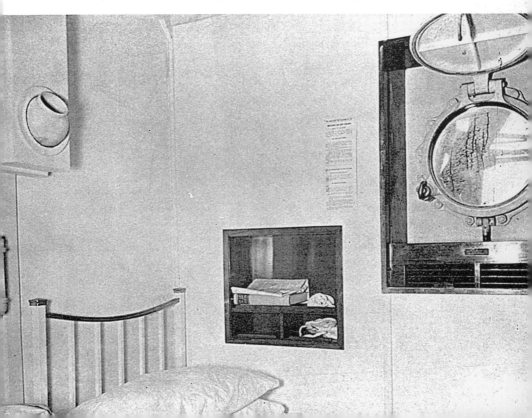

days after his medical examination, the steward happened to meet Steer in the washroom and, as they stood there side by side, Camb asked: "Have you said I was the man you saw in Cabin 126?"

"No," replied Steer, acting on the captain's orders.

"Thank goodness. I haven't been with her homeward bound this trip," said Camb, adding: "I'm in a tight jam."

It was soon after midnight on October 25 when the *Durban Castle* dropped anchor in Cowes Roads and at 1.25 the two waiting police officers went aboard. After talking to Captain Patey, the ship's surgeon, and other members of the crew, they inspected Gay Gibson's cabin. By the time it was James Camb's turn to be interviewed, four hours had elapsed.

"Have you ever been to Miss Gibson's cabin?" Detective Sergeant Patrick Quinlan asked.

"Never," said the steward.

Quinlan asked to see his wrists. Rolling up his sleeves, Camb explained: "I nearly scratched myself to death in my sleep in the night."

Quinlan's colleague, a detective constable, expressed his doubts that the wounds displayed could have been self-inflicted, to which Camb responded that he had done the same thing to the insides of his legs. But the officers were not that easily persuaded.

"I have reason to believe," said Quinlan, "that you can give me further information regarding this matter. I have also reason to believe that you were in Miss Gibson's cabin at about 3 a.m. in the early hours of the morning of October 18."

For the first time Camb began to suspect that Steer had revealed his identity to Captain Patey after all.

"That puts me in a tight spot," he commented.

When finally the *Durban Castle* docked at Southampton, Camb was immediately taken off to the police headquarters for further questioning, while a large team of detectives went on board the liner. Their activity centred on Cabin 126, where Gay Gibson's belongings were thoroughly searched for clues, the porthole was removed and closely examined and the door taken off its hinges and checked for fingerprints. At Quinlan's request, Miss Field arranged the bedclothes to resemble as closely as possible the state they were in when she first entered the cabin on the morning of October 18. As she did so, the CID officers noticed some stains on the top and bottom sheets, some of which appeared to have been caused by urine.

Later that day, Quinlan was back in the police station interview room, where he confronted Camb with the news that they knew beyond doubt that he was in Gay Gibson's cabin at 3 a.m.

"I want to tell you something. I did not want to tell you this morning in front of Mr Turner," responded the steward, referring to the presence at the earlier interview of a Union Castle representative, "as I had no right to go to her cabin, but I did go about eleven o'clock that night to ask her if she wanted some lemonade with her rum. I saw her in her cabin. She was looking through her luggage for a swimsuit, but she told me she could not find it. She went back upstairs, telling me to leave the rum in the usual place."

Asked about the suggestion that he had told Miss Gibson in the Long Gallery the previous evening that he had a bone to pick with her, Camb agreed and explained that he was aggrieved because he had prepared her tea tray that afternoon as usual but that she had not sent for it.

Camb was next informed that fragments of material had been found around the porthole suggesting that Miss Gibson had been pushed through it. He was also warned that if he persisted in his denials, any explanation that he might want to offer later would be difficult to accept.

"You mean," asked Camb, "that Miss Gibson might have died of some cause other than being murdered? She might have had a heart attack or something?"

It was an interesting question, but the interview quickly moved on as Detective Sergeant Quinlan asked Camb if he made a habit of visiting passengers in their cabins.

"Well, yes," boasted the steward. "Some of them like us better than the passengers. I've been with them several times on other trips."

"Was that at night?" Quinlan inquired.

"Yes," he said. "I've been with several. Of course, if I was found out I would get the sack."

The questioning continued until 7 p.m., at which point the investigation into Miss Gibson's disappearance took a new and dramatic turn. After being told once again that the police were absolutely certain that he was the last person to see her, Camb suddenly sat back in his chair and announced that he now wished to make a short statement. It was a document destined to be of crucial significance at his trial.

"I went to Miss Gibson's cabin at about 11 o'clock," said the dictated statement, "and during the course of the conversation with her I made an appointment to meet her that night. I knocked at the door after I had finished work at about 1 o'clock, but there was no answer. I opened the door of her cabin and found it was empty. I then went forward to the well deck, where I sat for about half-an-hour smoking. I then returned to Miss Gibson's cabin at about 2 o'clock and found her there. After a short conversation I got into bed with her consent. Intimacy took place. Whilst in the act of sexual intercourse she clutched me, foaming at the mouth. I immediately ceased the act, but she was very still. I felt for her heart beats, but could not find any. She was at that time very still, and I cannot offer any explanation as to how the bells came to be rung, as I most definitely did not touch them myself. Thinking she had fainted, I tried artificial respiration on her. Whilst doing this the night-watchman knocked at the door and attempted to open it. I shut the door again, saying it was all right. Then I panicked, as I thought he had gone to the bridge to report to the officer of the watch, as I did not want to be found in such a compromising position. I bolted the door and again tried artificial respiration. After a few minutes I could not find a sign of life. After a struggle with the limp body – by the way, she was still wearing her dressing gown – I managed to lift her to the porthole and push her through. I am fairly certain that at the time she was dead, but I was terribly frightened. I then went forward and turned in. The time would be about 3.30 a.m."

After reading over the statement and signing it, Camb commented that he was glad to have got it off his mind. Then, as an afterthought, he asked suddenly: "What will happen about this? My wife must not know about this. If she does I'll do away with myself."

It was a naive comment that suggested that Camb had still not grasped the seriousness of his plight. He was on the verge of being charged with committing a capital offence, yet he appeared to believe that it might still be possible to keep the matter from his wife. Further evidence of his lack of perception of his position followed when, on October 26, the charge of murder was formally preferred.

"My God!" he exclaimed. "I didn't think it was as serious as this!"

They were comments that his defence lawyers were later to offer as evidence of his innocence of the crime of murder.

While Camb was being interviewed at Southampton police headquarters, forensic experts were continuing their examination of Cabin 126 and its contents. Their discoveries included smears of human blood and traces of saliva and lipstick on the top sheet, and a single smear of blood on the bottom one. This evidence was consistent with death by strangulation, features of which often

Right: The front page of the *Southern Daily Echo* on the first day of Camb's trial. Pictures of Camb and Gay Gibson are also shown.

Below: The porthole from Cabin 126 is carried into court.

include frothing at the mouth and the discharge of flecks of blood. However, laboratory tests produced no evidence of the urine stains that would also have been expected if Gay Gibson had been strangled.

James Camb made his first appearance at a crowded Southampton magistrates' court on October 27. The hearing lasted just four minutes and he was remanded in custody. Committal proceedings began three weeks later but the trial was delayed until March, 1948, at the request of the defence, who wished to make inquiries in South Africa and perhaps arrange for witnesses to be brought over.

The trial finally opened at the Winchester Assizes on March 18 before Mr Justice Hilbery. Winchester Castle was undergoing major structural repairs at the time and the case was heard in a makeshift courtroom of canvas and plywood erected within the Great Hall. Only fifty-five seats were available to the public and they were occupied almost as soon as the courtroom opened, far more people being unable to obtain admission. Thirty reporters were also present, some of them from newspapers in South Africa, where the case had generated almost as much interest as it had in Britain. In the well of the temporary courtroom was a reconstruction of the *Durban Castle*'s Cabin 126, including the white-enamelled bedstead (exhibit 13) in which Gay Gibson had slept during the last few days of her life, and in which she probably died. Also among the exhibits on display were the bell-panel and the push-buttons that Camb denied either he or Miss Gibson had pressed on the fateful night, the cabin door, and also the porthole, which had been mounted in a wooden frame. Mr G.D. "Khaki" Roberts, K.C., led for the prosecution, Mr J.D. Casswell, K.C., for the defence. Soon after 10.30, James Camb was led into court.

"He was wearing a well-cut navy blue suit and it was not difficult to understand why he was attractive to a certain kind of woman," recalls Casswell in his memoirs. "Although he seemed unusually pale, his manner was composed and he made his plea of not guilty in a voice which gave no indication of internal strain. He had been waiting in prison nearly five months for this trial, and I think he was now almost glad that his ordeal, so long awaited, was about to begin."

In his opening speech, Roberts put forward two theories for the jury of nine men and three women to consider. The first was that Gay Gibson, having rejected Camb's advances, had pressed both bells to summon help, that she had scratched him, and that he had strangled her and forced her body through the porthole as the ship steamed northwards some ninety miles from the coast of West Africa. The second and alternative theory was that, having overcome the young woman's resistance, he had pushed her through the porthole while she was still alive.

"To some extent," counsel continued, "this is an unusual case, because there is no body here, no *corpus delicti*, as the lawyers say. That is unusual, but by no means unprecedented. Unfortunately there will be no doubt at all that Eileen Gibson is dead."

After summarizing Gay Gibson's life and career, Roberts went on to describe the location of Cabin 126 and Camb's duties as a first-class deck steward. He also spoke of Camb's attraction to – or interest in – Gay Gibson and gave a detailed chronological account of events leading up to and following the actress's disappearance.

The prosecution witnesses included the dead girl's mother, Mrs Ellen Gibson, who had travelled from South Africa with her husband and two grown-up sons. She spoke in glowing terms of her daughter, whom she described as "one of the finest types of English womanhood – physically, mentally and morally". But defence counsel Joshua Casswell had other ideas.

"Did you know that your daughter consulted Dr Schoub on grounds of her pregnancy?" he asked during cross-examination.

"My daughter was not pregnant, sir," Mrs Gibson asserted, firmly.

"Did you know your daughter was going about with several different men in Johannesburg?"

"She was not."

"Can you explain the contraceptive found in her case?"

"University students carry contraceptives, don't they?"

Casswell named several men with whom it was suggested that Gay had been friendly. Mrs Gibson denied knowledge of any of them.

"Did you hear the name of Shan Sventusky?" he asked.

"She knew him for about a fortnight."

"Do you know he sent flowers every night and took her away from the theatre every night?"

"I know he sent her flowers. I was away."

Questioned further, Mrs Gibson agreed that it was Sventusky who paid her daughter's first-class fare to England (£150) and that he had also given her £350. Asked why he had given the young woman so much money, she said it was because he was interested in her career.

"Did you approve of her receiving £500 from a man she had only known for a short time?" asked Casswell.

"It was a business proposition. He was a very successful businessman."

"Did you know she was telling everyone she was pregnant at that time?"

"She was not. I was a nurse and my daughter and I were very close friends. We had no secrets from one another."

"Would it be right to describe your daughter as neurotic, highly-strung and a very emotional girl?"

"No. She was very calm and controlled, with dignity and poise."

"Was she drinking heavily and, among other things, vodka?"

"No."

"In fact," concluded Casswell, "anything I might put to you against your daughter you would not believe for a single moment?"

"That is quite correct. One's daughter doesn't change in a fortnight after 21 years of honourable and conscientious living."

In his own account of the trial, written after his retirement, Casswell says that there was no more unpleasant moment for him than that when he rose to question Mrs Gibson. She was, he recalls, a "pleasant, round-faced, middle-aged Englishwoman, just like millions of other English mothers, with the same pride and the same loyalties". But in his view Gay Gibson was "not only not hostile to the advances of the opposite sex, but had on occasions even been the first to make the approach"; and it was his unpleasant task to "tear the shreds of self-deception about her only daughter from this woman for whom one could have only sympathy".

Later the same day, the second day of the trial, James Camb himself stepped into the witness box. He gave his evidence clearly and without hesitation, even when subjected to cross-examination. In fact, his composure was such that "Khaki" Roberts used it against him in his closing speech to the jury later in the trial.

"Camb says he threw her through the porthole in a panic," he barked. "Did he panic? Do you think he is the sort of man to panic? Members of the jury, did you notice him in the witness box last Saturday? The greatest ordeal that a man can undergo, giving evidence on a charge of murder, is being cross-examined. Did you see any sign of panic at all? Did you see any lack of poise or composure or full control of the thinking facilities?"

A crucial element of Camb's evidence was his claim that he and Gay Gibson were on "extremely friendly terms".

"When did the idea first occur to you of going to Miss Gibson's cabin?" asked Mr J.T. Malony, junior counsel for the defence.

"Soon after she left me in the Long Gallery in the evening," Camb replied.

"After five minutes I went down to her cabin to inquire whether she would want her supper tray or some lemonade to take with the rum. I said in a half-joking manner: 'I've a good mind to bring a drink down and join you'."

The judge asked: "What made you make that observation?"

"It's hard to say. She was so friendly by that time."

"What was it intended to convey?"

"I think I intended to convey what really happened later."

"What was her answer?"

"I am not certain of her exact words, but I believe she said: 'Please yourself – it's up to you'."

Camb then described what happened after he went to Cabin 126 in the early hours of October 18. The only light on in the cabin was the small bed-light. The actress was wearing a yellow quilted dressing gown. She lay back on the bed, sipping her rum, while he sat on the edge of it. They stayed like that for ten or fifteen minutes, discussing the dullness of the ship's dance that evening.

"Then," said Camb, "I reclined on the bed beside her."

"Did she object?" asked Malony.

"No, sir," said Camb, adding that "a certain amount of preliminary love-play" followed, and then sexual intercourse. He went on: "Just as intercourse would normally have come to an end, she suddenly heaved under me as though she was gasping for breath, as though she was taking a deep breath. Her body stiffened for the fraction of a second and then relaxed completely limp. Her right arm was still round my neck when she heaved against me. That arm automatically tightened, and the left hand, holding my right forearm, gripped tightly. All this happened in a matter of seconds. I immediately got off the bed. She was completely relaxed, as though she was in a dead faint, one eye just slightly open. Her mouth was a little open too. There was a faint line of bubbles – I assumed it to be froth – just on the edges of the lips. It was a muddy colour and appeared to be slightly blood-flecked. I was rather stunned for the moment. First of all I listened and felt for her heart beats. I could not find any and I attempted by massaging the stomach towards the heart to bring back circulation. I tried for twenty or twenty-five minutes to revive her."

Questioned again by Mr Justice Hilbery, Camb said he was standing by the bed as he tried to revive Gay Gibson. It was at this time, according to the defence counsel, that his hip probably touched the bell-buttons and, though he was not aware of it until Steer appeared at the cabin door, alerted the nightwatchmen in the A deck galley.

Mrs Ellen Gibson, the actress's mother. *(Photo: Southern Daily Echo)*

Above: The courtroom reconstruction of Gay Gibson's cabin.

Below: Defence witnesses Henry Gilbert and his wife Dr Ina Schoub. *(Photo: Southern Daily Echo)*

Camb continued: "I was in a complete state of panic – afraid of being found in the cabin. I knew that being found in a lady's cabin, I would lose my job and forfeit any chance of re-employment in any shipping company. I concluded she was dead. I had no doubt in my mind and I have no doubt now. I confess now that it sounds very foolish but I hoped to give the impression that she had fallen overboard and to deny knowledge of having been in the cabin, in the hope that the captain's inquiries would not be too severe. I decided to dispose of the body by pushing it through the porthole. I lifted her up and pushed her through. The body was so slack and rather awkward."

Not surprisingly, James Camb faced a searching cross-examination by "Khaki" Roberts. He was forced to admit that he had lied consistently up to the time when he realized that he had been positiviely identified as the person seen in Cabin 126. He also conceded that he had never heard of such a terrible happening at sea as a member of the crew of a British ship throwing a lady passenger through a porthole.

"You knew there was not the slightest chance of the body being recovered?" Roberts asked.

"I believe so, sir."

"You realise the body of a dead person is the most valuable evidence of the cause of death?"

"Yes, sir."

"If your second story – the story you are telling now – is true, you destroyed the best evidence in your favour, did you not?"

"I didn't think of that at the time."

"If your second story is as false as your first, you destroyed the most deadly evidence against you, didn't you?"

"Yes, sir."

It was incisive questioning, perhaps decisive, but Camb struggled on. After half-an-hour, he was briefly re-examined by Joshua Casswell.

"Are you proud of what you did that night?" the defence counsel asked.

"I am not, sir. I am ashamed," Camb replied.

The trial went on for four days and, as the *Southern Daily Echo* put it, every moment of it was a "dour struggle directed by two of the country's most eminent King's Counsel". A key witness for the defence was the pathologist James Webster, Director of the West Midland Forensic Science Laboratory in Birmingham. Webster testified that the evidence presented to him was certainly consistent with death by strangulation but it was also consistent with death from heart failure during sexual intercourse. He said he had personal knowledge of three cases in which young people, in whom there were no signs of a condition that might have caused death, had died during intimacy.

"The account given of this girl's death could have occurred," Webster told the court.

He added that a history of asthma, bluish lips, fingernails changing colour and fainting – all symptoms that the defence claimed Gay Gibson had shown – would be consistent with heart trouble.

Other defence witnesses included Henry Gilbert, producer of the Johannesburg production of *Golden Boy*, his wife, who practised medicine as Dr Ina Schoub, and Mike Abel, who, like Gay Gibson, was a member of the cast of Gilbert's production. Both men spoke of occasions when Gay had had hysterical attacks or had fainted during parties and on one occasion in the street. Abel said that once she asked him for £200 to get back to England, as she was pregnant and had no faith in South African doctors. She also told him she was asthmatic. Another time, in his car, she caught his arm and told him she loved him. He told her not to be so silly and she became excited and fainted, white saliva appearing at the corners of her mouth. Gilbert said that Gay came to him one day and said she was "terribly unhappy", that she could not love like other people, that she was not like other girls. She seemed to be perturbed about sex and it was because of this that he introduced her to his wife. Dr Schoub said Gay told her she had had sexual experience and was worried that she might be pregnant.

"What sort of picture," Casswell asks in his memoirs, "does all this evidence conjure up? This temperamental, semi-hysterical young woman, complaining of asthmatic attacks, on occasions short of breath and experiencing difficulties in breathing, telling a married man that she loved him, boasting of her involvements with two other men, and confessing openly to probable pregnancy?"

He adds that having personally interviewed the defence witnesses before the trial, he was not only satisfied that their accounts of Gay Gibson's health and behaviour were genuine but had found that they were prepared to give evidence unfavourable to her reputation only when assured that a man's life might depend on their testimonies. Nevertheless, having completed his own summing up, and listened to those of Roberts and the Judge, Casswell was not optimistic as, at 6.25 p.m. on Monday March 22, the jury retired to consider its verdict.

"Mr Justice Hilbery summed up in a way which, while well within the bounds of judicial propriety, can only be described as unfavourable to the accused," he says.

The jury returned after forty-six minutes and most of the jurors kept their heads bowed as the foreman announced that they had found the defendant guilty of murder. Camb himself, whose face up to this moment had appeared slightly flushed, seemed to pale and his eyes dropped. Asked if he had anything to say why judgement of death should not be passed, he raised his head and looked the judge straight in the eye.

"My Lord," he said. "At the opening of this case I was asked to plead guilty or not guilty. I pleaded not guilty and I repeat that statement now."

"His words rang clear through the tent-like court within the Great Hall of Winchester Castle," reported the *Southern Daily Echo*. "Those standing in the hall itself, outside the temporary courtroom, could hear his words quite clearly. The judge's clerk balanced the square piece of black cloth, which his lordship had carried into court each day, on the Judge's wig and said: 'His lordship commands all persons to stand.' In cold, unimpassioned tones, in a hushed court, Mr Justice Hilbery, his gaunt features recording none of the emotion he must have felt, repeated the words of the death sentence."

One person who was not present to hear the verdict was Camb's wife, Margaret. She did not appear in Winchester at all during the trial but stayed throughout at a friend's house near Southampton, convinced that her husband would be acquitted and awaiting a reunion with him. "News had to be sent to her there of the jury's adverse verdict," said the *Echo* report.

Tuesday April 13 was the date fixed for Camb's execution, but on April 1 it was announced that an appeal had been lodged against the conviction on the grounds that the jury had been misdirected. It was heard at the Court of Criminal Appeal on April 26, and dismissed.

"It seems to me," commented the Lord Chief Justice, Lord Goddard, "that the evidence on which the jury returned their verdict might almost be described as overwhelming."

By this time a petition launched by Southampton businessman A.P.G. Elson, calling for a reprieve for Camb, had attracted thousands of signatures from people in Britain, South Africa, and elsewhere. In the event it was not needed, for Parliament was currently debating the abolition of capital punishment and the Home Secretary, Chuter Ede, considered that in the circumstances anyone under sentence of death should have his sentence commuted to life imprisonment.

Eight months later, at a divorce court in Southampton, 28-year-old Mrs Margaret Camb was granted a decree nisi against her husband. The next time the couple met was in 1959, when she travelled to Wakefield Prison in Yorkshire, from which he was soon to be released on licence after almost twelve years as a model prisoner. The purpose of her visit was to persuade Camb to sign papers agreeing not to approach her or their child, now aged fourteen, after his release. Camb willingly signed. Whatever he might now feel about his wife and child, his main objective was to use his forthcoming freedom to prove his innocence.

"My son still feels badly about the verdict," said his elderly father, Robert Camb. "Ever since he was sentenced he has maintained that he was innocent. He had nothing at all to gain by telling me that story, but he has stuck to it and I believe him. He says he would not have been convicted if other witnesses had come forward, and he is sure that he can clear his name by finding them."

In support of his claims, Camb wrote a series of newspaper articles, published in 1959, soon after his release. He also retained the sympathy of the barrister who had led his defence.

"I must say that I am not convinced of his guilt," wrote Casswell in his book. "I think the evidence did not justify his conviction. I was inclined to think at the time that my client's story was true and on balance I still think so today."

Camb never did succeed in his attempts to prove his innocence. In fact, his credibility suffered a further setback in 1971 when, having changed his name by deed poll to James Clarke, he appeared in court in Scotland and pleaded guilty to using "lewd, indecent and libidinous practices towards three girls", two aged eleven, the other aged ten. The girls were guests at the Waverley Castle Hotel, Melrose, where the former *Durban Castle* steward was employed as head waiter. He was sentenced to three years imprisonment and to resume his life sentence for the murder of Gay Gibson.

It was not the first time Camb had been accused of offences of a sexual nature. Inquiries with the South African police following Gay Gibson's disappearance had revealed details of three assaults allegedly committed on teenage girls on board the *Durban Castle* between September 11, 1947, when she left Southampton for Durban, and October 10, when she left on the homeward journey that was to have such a tragic outcome. The incidents were not, of course, mentioned at Camb's trial because of their obviously prejudicial nature.

Something else not aired at the trial was the fact that no signs were found on Gay Gibson's bedclothes, to show that sexual intercourse had taken place. Had Camb been facing a rape charge, this would have been a powerful point in his favour. But a cornerstone of his defence was that intercourse did take place and evidence to the contrary would surely have sealed his fate rather sooner had it not, as "Khaki" Roberts admits in his memoirs, been overlooked by counsel for the prosecution.

9
THE FATAL PICNIC
The murders of Lydia and Norma Leakey in 1956

It was warm and sunny on the afternoon of Sunday June 17, 1956, as a Wolseley car and its three occupants headed out of Poole in Dorset and towards the Hampshire border. At the wheel was big and brawny Albert Goozee, a 32-year-old fitter's mate and former merchant seaman; in the passenger seats were his former landlady, Mrs. Lydia Leakey, who was 53, and her 14-year-old daughter, Norma. The trio were going on a picnic in the New Forest. The weather was ideal for their little adventure and so was the proposed setting in Bignell Wood, near Cadnam. In other circumstances, it could hardly have failed to be a perfect afternoon. But the picnickers were no ordinary threesome. They were, as a senior detective was later to observe, involved in a "love-hate triangle" that could only end in disaster. As they travelled through the leafy New Forest lanes, that disaster was only hours away. Before the afternoon was over, Lydia and Norma would be dead and Goozee in hospital with knife wounds.

The seeds of the tragedy had been sown almost eighteen months earlier, soon after Goozee, in January 1955, became a lodger in the Leakey family's semi-detached house in Alexandra Road, Parkstone, Poole.

"It happened," recalls the then head of Hampshire CID, Detective Chief Superintendent Walter Jones, in an autobiographical account of his career, "during a birthday party for Norma Leakey on February 4. Goozee, Mrs. Leakey and Norma had been drinking red wine, and began playing a game of Spin the Bottle — a kind of Postman's Knock — which ended with Goozee being obliged by the rules of the game to go outside and give Lydia Leakey a kiss. According to Goozee, he was joined in his lodger's bed that night first by Lydia Leakey and, later, by Norma as well."

During his stay with the Leakeys, Goozee changed his job several times, working as a bus conductor (from which he was sacked for being too familiar with female passengers), a roundsman and a labourer. He also joined the army in December 1955 but bought himself out after two months.

Goozee's relationships with his landlady and her daughter progressed rapidly, but it was a fraught situation. Lydia Leakey's disabled husband, Tom, a wood machine operator and former employee of the chemical company British Drug Houses, also lived in the house, although the couple had not enjoyed marital relations for some years, apparently on medical advice. Leakey, who had lost a leg during World War I, slept in the back bedroom, Goozee occupied the middle room, and Lydia and her daughter shared the front room.

Although Lydia Leakey, a needleworker and former laundry hand at the Primrose Laundry, Parkstone, did not survive to tell her version of the story, there seems no doubt that she was having a sexual relationship with Goozee. He discussed the affair from time to time with others, including another daughter of the Leakeys, Mrs Mary Hayward, and his brother, Thomas Goozee, and after the tragedy he made no attempt to hide that he had been "carrying on" with Lydia and that they had slept together. He claimed he had only had to leave his bedroom door open at night for Lydia to come and join him.

The exact nature of Goozee's relationship with Norma — described by friends as a "rather shy and nervous" girl, with an interest in ballet — is less certain. According to Goozee's own account, the Parkstone Grammar School pupil, the youngest of four children and the only one still living at home, was aware of what was going on between him and her mother and demanded that he devote the same attention to her, he later told police. "I was carrying on with the mother, sleeping with her. Her daughter wanted me to do the same to her. She got all hysterical. The daughter has turned me into a sex maniac."

Not surprisingly, Goozee's presence and the developing relationships caused a certain amount of domestic disturbance within the Leakey household. On one occasion, according to Tom Leakey, Goozee came downstairs "raving with temper" and accused his landlady of carrying on with men during the war. The following day, Leakey challenged the lodger, accusing him of having an affair with his wife. Goozee denied it, saying: "No, of course not, Tom. Who told you that?"

The lodger offered to leave the house but was told he could stay if he behaved himself. He did stay but the next dispute between the men was more serious. It followed a remark made by Goozee who, referring to the difficulties between Tom and Lydia Leakey, announced that he had "made it all right between you and Mum". Leakey, clearly irritated by the comment, told Goozee that he had had no relations with Lydia for seven years or so and he did not want him making arrangements between him and his wife. The incident ended with Goozee knocking Leakey over the head, causing him to fall and break a table.

The following day, Leakey left his home and went to Enham Alamein, near Andover, to stay with his sister. While he was there he fell ill and the sister sent a telegram to Parkstone to let the family know. Goozee then drove Lydia and Norma Leakey to Andover, where there was a further confrontation.

According to Leakey, Goozee asked him: "I suppose you have told them I have hit you?" Leakey agreed and Goozee then said: "The next time I will kill you."

At this, Norma started crying and screaming and begged her aunt not to send for the police.

"He said he would get us if she did, Norma told us," said Leakey. He added that his sister picked up a poker, at which he himself went to fetch a policeman. An officer duly arrived but said that it was a domestic matter and that he could do nothing.

Leakey told his family that he would not return to Parkstone until Goozee had left the house in Alexandra Road. Goozee returned to Dorset alone and Lydia Leakey subsequently wrote a letter telling him: "We are coming back on Thursday, so Tom says you will have to be gone by then. I am sorry this has happened."

Leakey and his daughter walked to the post together but Norma refused to post the letter so her father did it himself. When, on the Thursday, they returned to Alexandra Road, Goozee was not there but later that day he did arrive and, according to Leakey, knocked him around again while his wife was next door.

"I called for help and he threatened to kill me. I picked up my stick to protect myself," the disabled Leakey recalled in the witness box at Hampshire Assizes months later.

Goozee finally left the house at the beginning of June 1956 and moved to new lodgings at the home of Mr and Mrs A.C. Pemberton, of Sunnyhill Road,

Parkstone. He told them they would find him a "good lodger", as he did not smoke or drink or keep late hours. In the short time he was with them, the couple did indeed have no complaints and found him, in Isobel Pemberton's words, to be a "nice, quiet man".

On Friday June 15, Goozee went with two friends to the New Royal Theatre in Bournemouth. He had four tickets for the last performance and at the theatre door offered the spare ticket to a woman and her 14-year-old daughter who had been unable to gain admission. At Goozee's suggestion, the girl sat alongside him and his friends, while her mother – who handed over 4s 6d for the ticket – stood at the back of the theatre, hoping that a second seat would become available at the interval.

Before the end of the performance, the mother suddenly saw her daughter running towards her in a distressed state. She claimed she had been sexually assaulted by Goozee, who soon found himself being interviewed by police in the manager's office. Later that night, he was charged with indecent assault and bailed to make a court appearance on the following Wednesday, June 20.

By the time Goozee returned to his lodgings, it was Saturday morning and he told Mrs Pemberton that he had been detained all night at the police station for a speeding offence. Later he left for work at the Tollard Royal Hotel on Bournemouth's West Cliff – coincidentally the same hotel in which the notorious double killer Neville Heath had stayed and in which he wined and dined his second victim, Doreen Marshall, before slaughtering her on the sands at Branksome Dene Chine in 1946.

According to Goozee, he was visited at the Tollard Royal on that third Saturday in June 1956 by Lydia Leakey – and it was not the first meeting between them since his expulsion from her house a couple of weeks earlier. In fact, Tom Leakey was later to testify that Goozee called at his former lodgings on several occasions during the intervening fortnight and picked up Lydia and Norma in his car. Exactly what passed between them during these meetings is uncertain but, according to Goozee's own account, Lydia was trying to blackmail him into returning to Alexandra Road by threatening to reveal that he had had a sexual relationship with her daughter.

On the morning of Sunday June 17, Goozee stayed in bed until lunchtime. When he did eventually get up, he went out almost immediately, telling his landlady he would be back for lunch at 2 o'clock. In the event he was back by 1.30, having been to see Lydia and Norma to make arrangements for the outing that afternoon.

Mrs Pemberton had prepared a traditional Sunday lunch for her lodger but he ate very little, complaining that he felt sick. The landlady administered an Alka Seltzer and Goozee went off to his room, saying that he was going to write a letter.

Mr Pemberton recalled: "He said he did not feel very grand. Then he said he thought he would take his car and go and 'have a blow' in the New Forest. He said the fresh air would do him good. He went upstairs to get his portable radio and went off at about two to 2.30 p.m. That was the last we saw of him."

Goozee drove straight to Alexandra Road to collect Lydia and Norma. They loaded the items for the picnic along with, at Lydia's suggestion according to Goozee, an axe, and and some wood to make a campfire. Tom Leakey had gone out for a drink and when he came home he found a curious note awaiting him. "I wanted to go for a ride, Daddy – love Norma," it read. Yet it was clear from the handwriting that it had been written by Lydia Leakey.

The trio set off on their fateful trip to the New Forest, Albert Goozee at the wheel of the black Wolseley, Lydia Leakey sitting beside him in the front passenger seat, Norma in the back. On their way through the forest, they stopped for a short time at the Rufus Stone, which is supposed to mark the spot where William Rufus, King of England and third son of William the Conqueror, was killed by an arrow in 1100. Norma wanted to see the monument in connection with an I-spy competition in a newspaper. Soon after resuming their journey, they turned off the metalled road and on to a muddy track. The track led to Canterton Glen, near the Bignell Wood cottage once occupied by Sir Arthur Conan Doyle, the creator of Sherlock Holmes, and it was here that the party decided to have their picnic.

According to Goozee, the mother and daughter went for a walk while he lit a fire, put a kettle on it and put tea in the teapot. "Mrs Leakey and Norma came back from a walk down the path," he told the jury at the Hampshire Assizes. "I had my jacket off and I was squatting down in front of the fire with the kettle. Mrs Leakey then spoke to Norma again and suggested that she went for another walk. The young girl asked her mother how long she should be away and I answered that the kettle would take at least ten to fifteen minutes to boil. Norma went away and Mrs Leakey then asked me why I didn't come round and try to make things up with Tom and if we couldn't carry on like we used to. She told me that she was very unhappy without me at the house and that she was very unhappy when I left. I said I would not come back and I didn't want her to worry me. Then Mrs Leakey asked me if I would just be friends with her and if I would have sexual intercourse with her for the last time. The way she was acting was very strange."

Goozee claimed that he then took his coat from the car and produced a letter he had written earlier, addressed to the Chief Constable of Bournemouth. The letter gave an account of his relationships with the mother and daughter and went on: "I was told to leave the house ... and I did, but Mrs Leakey still comes after me so I have come to the only possible way out before I go after another young girl. Please do not put too much trouble on my brother because he knows how Mrs Leakey and Norma went after me. I went into the army to try to get away from it all but once you have messed about with a young girl there is not much you can do for yourself."

At the Assize Court, Goozee continued: "I showed Mrs Leakey this letter and told her I was absolutely fed up with what she was doing and I was not enjoying having sexual intercourse with a woman old enough to be my mother. She then promised me that if I would give in, it would never happen again. I told her that if she did ever worry me that I would rather do three or four years in prison than have her keep saying I had had sexual intercourse with Norma. With that we started to kiss each other."

But, in Goozee's version of the events that followed, Norma returned to the picnic spot 'too soon'. As he and her mother sat together on a blanket, the 14-year-old came up behind them with an axe, hit her mother on the head with it and then became hysterical, screaming: "You beast, why don't you leave Albert alone?"

Goozee claimed he hit Norma on the face twice, then bundled her into the back of the car. He saw that Lydia Leakey – by now sitting on the front passenger seat with her feet on the ground outside the car – had a knife in her hand and he tried to take it from her. In doing so, Goozee said, he slipped and felt the knife penetrate his side.

"I thought my life was finished, so I jabbed the knife in her," he told police. "Norma came out of the car and came at me, screaming, 'What have you done to my mother? Why don't you do the same to me?' After that my mind must have gone blank. I don't remember stabbing Norma. I passed out. I came to about an hour later and they were both lying there. They were both dead so I got in the car and drove down in the direction I could hear the traffic."

Not long afterwards, a motorist and his passenger travelling along the Cadnam to Brook road about half-a-mile from Cadnam saw a man slumped over the mudguard of a car parked on the verge. They stopped and Goozee staggered over, clutching his stomach. While the driver went off to telephone for the police and an ambulance, Goozee made what amounted to a roadside confession to the passenger, carpenter John Hull, of Nomansland in the New Forest. "There's been a murder in the forest," he told him. "Two women have been stabbed. She attacked me with a knife and I killed them both."

Another motorist, Eric Fearn, of Eastleigh, arrived and Goozee told him: "Get me on my feet while I'm still alive and I'll take you to where the others are. There are two more in there – two women. They're both dead. I killed them." Asked what had happened, he added: "My landlady and her daughter. We were carrying on together. She stuck a knife in me, so I went for them and killed them. It's a long knife. It's in the back of the car."

The first detectives to arrive at the scene found the tin kettle still hanging on a car starting handle over the dying embers of Goozee's picnic fire. Nearby was the small aluminium teapot.   The bodies of the woman and girl were fully clothed. Lydia Leakey, whose watch had stopped at 4.20, had sustained two deep stab wounds on the left side of her stomach. There was also a gaping wound on her head, apparently inflicted by the blood-stained axe found beneath her body, and under the head wound her skull had been fractured.

Norma Leakey had two stab wounds to the heart, a broken cheek bone and jaw, and severe bruising to her head.

Detective Chief Superintendent Jones recalls: "Goozee's car was spattered with blood on the inside, on the rear window and over the seats. A pile of clothes on the back seat had been scattered about, indicating a violent struggle inside the car. Also on the back seat were a number of letters, including Goozee's note to the Bournemouth police. A search was made for the murder weapon – the knife with a blade six-and-a-half inches long – and it was found in the car's toolbox, under the offside bonnet."

The CID chief goes on: "The blade of the knife was covered in blood, and it was these bloodstains which made me suspicious of Goozee's story of the events leading up to the death of the two women. He had told of being stabbed and then, thinking he was dying, of having stabbed the knife into Mrs Leakey and finally Norma."

Jones had the knife sent to the Metropolitan Police laboratory at Scotland Yard, where tests showed that most of the blood on the blade was of Group O, which matched samples taken from Goozee in hospital. But Lydia Leakey and her daughter were both of Group A – and the only blood of that group on the knife was around the hilt.

First news of the New Forest double killing appears in the *Bournemouth Daily Echo*.

"It was likely therefore," adds Jones, "that the knife had first been used on the women and only then had it been plunged into Goozee ... Had his story been true, and had he used the knife on Lydia and Norma Leakey, after having been stabbed himself, it should have been *their* blood ... Group A ... which showed predominantly on the weapon."

Goozee was admitted to the Aldridge ward of the Royal South Hants Hospital, Southampton, where Jones interviewed him as soon as doctors pronounced him fit to be seen the following day. The detective found him to be a dark, swarthy man with dark eyes. He also found him to be "extremely talkative". When excited, he tended to wave his hands about and speak extremely rapidly, so much so that Detective Inspector Alf Stutchfield found it difficult to keep up with him when taking down his statement.

Goozee willingly told detectives his version of the story in great detail. He told of his affair with Lydia Leakey and his relationship with Norma; he told of the picnic outing to the New Forest and of the struggle that ended in the deaths of the woman and the girl.

"Are you sure you didn't stab yourself?" Jones asked him.

"No," replied Goozee. "I'm too much of a coward for that, sir."

"You have two other small cuts on the stomach," Jones pointed out.

"She pricked me twice when I was trying to get hold of the knife," was the explanation.

Jones asked Goozee how he accounted for the blood on the inside of the back of the car. Goozee thought for a few moments, then said: "Norma kept putting her hand to her mouth and flicking it away." He demonstrated with his hand, then repeated: "I remember it quite well now. She did it with her hand."

In his memoirs, Detective Chief Superintendent Jones notes: "I had him kept under constant observation in the hospital and, throughout the week he was there, he kept up an almost continuous stream of chatter, regardless of the detectives who sat at his bedside. Some of those pieces of conversation were written down and despite being warned that they might be used in evidence should he appear in court, Goozee gabbled on."

On his first night in hospital, Goozee woke up in the early hours and announced: "I have read about landladies and lodgers but I never thought it would happen to me. She knew I was seducing her daughter. What could I do? She bought me the car."

A few days later, he said: "Do I look insane? I will get away with it. She was getting what she wanted for two years. He led her a dog's life, the swine. Do you know that I could not leave my bedroom door open at night but she would come into bed with me? That's the worst of carrying on with the lodger. It only causes jealousy."

On June 23, Goozee told PC Norman Thompson: "The whole trouble was blackmail. I used to have to give the girl anything she asked for, records and so on, or else she would go straight to her father and tell about mother and me. If I get the chance I will do Leakey. He is the bastard who should be dead."

On another occasion, Goozee gazed from his hospital bed towards the night sister and observed: "She's nice. She's the only one I'd commit murder again for."

And six days after the Bignell Wood tragedy, he chose to talk about how easy it was to stab someone.

"It's so easy ... goes in like butter ... I thought that you would have to push in hard ... I think that was half the trouble," he said.

While Albert Goozee was beginning his stay in hospital, Lydia Leakey and her daughter were on their way to the mortuary. They were certified dead by Dr A.J. Dandy, of Minstead, a police surgeon, and identified by Tom Leakey. An inquest was opened at Lyndhurst police station on Wednesday June 20, when Dr R.A. Goodbody stated that the cause of Lydia Leakey's death was contusion of the brain due to a fracture of the skull by a blunt instrument and haemorrhage and shock from stab wounds in the abdomen. Norma had received a stab wound to the heart, he said, adding that both were alive when they were stabbed. The inquest was adjourned until October 1.

The first that Mr and Mrs Pemberton knew of the affair was when they read the front page lead story in the Monday June 18 issue of the *Bournemouth Daily Echo*. It was, said Isobel Pemberton, a "terrible shock" to learn of the involvement of the "nice, quiet man" who had been their lodger for two weeks.

Lydia and Norma Leakey were buried in a single grave at Poole Cemetery on June 23. Two hundred people turned out for the funeral and the wreaths included one from Albert Goozee's brother and sister-in-law from Oakdale, Poole. Some of Norma's schoolfriends from Parkstone Grammar School waited in uniform at the graveside.

Goozee made his first court appearance at Totton on June 26, charged with two murders, and was remanded until July 3. The *Echo* described him as "tall and slim and well groomed" and dressed in a pale blue American battledress–type summer suit. The report continued: "During the short proceedings, he sat opposite the magistrate, Mr G. H. Truckell, with his arms on the table between them and seemed to take a greater interest in his surroundings than in what was being said. He smiled broadly when he asked for bail, which was not granted."

Goozee was remanded again on June 10, 17 and 24 but on July 30, the prosecution was ready to begin committal proceedings at Southampton. The prosecution case was summarized by E. G. MacDermott, who also read a five-page statement alleged to have been made by Goozee describing his relationships with Lydia and Norma Leakey and giving his version of the killings. The prosecution witnesses included Tom Leakey, whose evidence of identification of his wife and daughter was interrupted by the defendant.

"It was not your daughter," Goozee shouted from the small, cage-like dock.

"You be quiet," retorted Mr Truckell.

The hearing was adjourned until Friday August 3, when evidence was called from additional police witnesses, including Constable M. Clarke, who related conversations he had had with Goozee within hours of the tragedy.

"It is a sexual matter. There are two women in the forest. They are both dead," the accused man told him. Later, in the ambulance on the way to hospital, he added: "She tried to kill me once before. One is the mother, the other is the daughter, 14 years. I was carrying on with the mother, sleeping with her. Her daughter wanted me to do the same to her. The daughter has made me a sex maniac. Then the husband got wise and wanted me out. I could take you to them. I stuck it [the knife] once into the daughter and then twice into the mother, I think. The daughter caused it. She got all hysterical."

Goozee told the court he did not wish to give evidence at the committal proceedings, nor did he wish to call any witnesses.

"I plead not guilty," he added, before being committed for trial at the next Hampshire Assizes.

The trial opened at Winchester on Monday December 3 before Mr Justice Havers and a jury of eight men and four women. As was the custom at that time, only one of the two murder charges was put to Goozee, in this case the killing of Norma Leakey, which he again denied. Mr N. R. Fox-Andrews, QC, opening the case for the prosecution, laid particular emphasis on Goozee's statements, especially one made to a surgeon in hospital in which he allegedly described how, during the argument in Bignell Wood, Lydia Leakey "came right at me and on to" the knife and how at that point "the daughter got all hysterical and I just did it to her as well". If the jury accepted that evidence, said Mr Fox-Andrews, and if they believed that the words meant that Goozee stuck the knife into the daughter, then in his view they could come to only one verdict.

"According to that statement, the order of events was this," argued the prosecution counsel. "He was stabbed by the mother first. He then either stabbed the mother or she ran accidentally on to the knife. Thirdly, according to that statement, he stabbed the daughter."

Mr Fox-Andrews said Goozee then made another statement to the doctor which, in the light of his claim that he was stabbed first, was "very peculiar". He said to the doctor: "Won't gangreen have set in with three kinds of blood in me?"

Mr Fox-Andrews asked the jury: "If he had been stabbed first, how many kinds of blood would there have been in him? The answer could be none except his own. On that account of his, there would be no possibility of the blood of either of the women being in him."

The key prosecution witnesses included Tom Leakey, who again described the complex relationships within the household as seen from his standpoint, and also the confrontations between him and Goozee who, he said, had twice threatened to kill him.

Late on the second day of the trial, Goozee gave evidence. He recalled how he came to share a bed with Lydia Leakey for the first time after the birthday party when they had played Spin the Bottle. Goozee began to explain the rules of the game at some length, prompting an apologetic comment from his counsel, Robert Hughes, who told the judge: "He thinks it is important – I don't want to stop him, my lord."

Goozee told the court that during the game, a child spun the bottle and it pointed to Mrs Leakey, and when she in her turn spun the bottle, "by some unknown fate" it pointed to him. By the rules of the game, this meant he had to go out into the passage and kiss Mrs Leakey, who told him she had been "longing to do this for the fortnight you have been here".

Later that evening, between 11.30 and midnight, after Goozee had retired for the night, Lydia Leakey came into his room in her nightclothes, sat on the bed, and began to tell him what a bad life she had had with her husband. Goozee said he realized "from the way she was going on" that she was "leading up to something". At first, he claimed, he did not agree to what Mrs Leakey wanted but then he became afraid of a scene and of rousing her husband. Then Norma came into the bedroom and all three of them finished up in the same bed.

"I am not quite sure what the arrangement is now," cut in Mr Justice Havers.

"Would you like me to draw you a plan?" Goozee asked.

"Oh, no," replied the judge.

Goozee said his relationship with Lydia continued for about nine months, after which he moved to other lodgings. He soon returned because she was blackmailing him to do so under the threat that she would tell the police he had been playing about with Norma. He later bought himself out of the army for the same reason, with Lydia providing £28 of the required £30 and her husband giving the remaining £2.

"I was getting a letter from her nearly every day. She was begging me to come back, saying she was going to be a mother to me, and doing away with all the sex," he said.

But the sex was not done away with and the sleeping arrangements resumed as before. He said he shared a bed with both mother and daughter but claimed that he never had intercourse with the fourteen-year-old. But the girl went everywhere with him. They went on cycle trips together, they visited Downton and Salisbury and they even spent a night in a double room at a Salisbury hotel, checking in as "Mr Goozee and Miss Goozee" – father and daughter.

Continuing his evidence the following morning, Goozee stunned everyone involved in the case, including his own counsel, by describing a sequence of events in Bignell Wood that none of them had heard before. He now claimed not only that it was Norma who hit Lydia on the head with the axe but that it was Lydia and not himself who stabbed Norma. Referring to the moment when Lydia was sitting in the front seat of the car, Goozee told the court: "I put Norma in the back of the car and told her not to worry. I then went round to Mrs Leakey. She was quite all right, but blood was coming from her head. The handkerchief you see with all the blood on was the handkerchief I used for wiping Mrs Leakey's neck, trying to clear the blood away to see the extent of the damage which was caused by the axe. I then told Mrs Leakey that now she had this wound, the whole matter would have to come before the police. Mrs Leakey then went like a mad woman. This knife was in her hand, and I struggled with Mrs Leakey for the knife. The knife pierced my chest a couple of times. I hadn't seen Norma get out of the car. I was still struggling with Mrs Leakey and then I felt the knife go into my side. I was very weak then and Norma came between me and her mother. I saw Mrs Leakey lunge at Norma. I couldn't do anything to prevent it. As far as I can remember I only saw the knife go into the girl's breast. Mrs Leakey was like a raving maniac. Norma was staggering."

Mr Hughes asked: "Did you stab Norma at all?"

"I never touched Norma with the knife. I was struggling with Mrs Leakey. I got her wrist and I turned the knife into her stomach. I think Mrs Leakey was stabbed twice."

The track leading to Canterton Glen, where the bodies were found. *(Photo: Bournemouth Daily Echo)*

Goozee said Lydia stumbled away from him and at that moment he collapsed. When he came to much later, he saw the woman and girl lying on the ground beside the car, apparently dead.

"I must have put the rug over the women," he said. "I was very sorry for what I could see then and I picked the knife up and tried to push the knife deeper into the wound that was already still there. I collapsed again and when I came to the knife was still sticking in me."

Asked if he had told the story to anyone before, Goozee said he had told it to a Roman Catholic priest in Winchester Prison the previous Sunday.

In his summing up for the defence, Mr Hughes described Goozee's latest version as a "very eleventh hour story" which had "come as a surprise even to those defending him". He was also forced to admit, by implication, that the development had thrown the defence strategy as originally planned into some disarray. Earlier in the trial, Mr Hughes had told the jury he would be urging them to bring in a verdict of manslaughter on the grounds that provocation on the part of Mrs Leakey had "caused a sudden and temporary loss of self-control, rendering the accused so subject to passion as to make him for the moment not master of his own mind".

Now he urged them: "Forget all about manslaughter or provocation. Let me start with a clean sheet. The issues now, as I see them, are: 'Is this man guilty of murder or is he not guilty?' So far as I see it, there is no halfway house."

Mr Hughes agreed that Goozee had told a "welter of lies". "But although he has admitted to having told a number of lies, it would not be right to dismiss the whole of his story on the basis that he had lied here and there," he said. "Although it was only today that we heard what he now says are the true facts of the case, two points may impress you. Who was the man to whom Goozee first made what he says is the true statement? He said it was to a priest last Sunday. And when he tells the story from the witness box, the situation is quite different from everything he said before – at the roadside, at the hospital, from everything he said in the statement to the police or any statement he might have made to his legal advisers."

Continuing his gallant attempt to turn a potentially disastrous blunder by his client into a case-winning masterstroke, Mr Hughes added: "When he gave evidence in the witness box, he was giving it on oath. That is the difference between Goozee's story today and everything else he said beforehand."

The jury retired at 3.25 p.m. on the fourth day of the trial, taking with them, at their own request, Goozee's pullover with stab holes in it, the eight-inch-long commando knife, and copies of the statements. Each juror also carried an album of photographs taken at the scene of the tragic picnic.

Two-and-a-quarter hours into their retirement, the jury asked for more exhibits to be taken to them, including Norma Leakey's blood-stained brassiere. This request was granted but two requests for tea were turned down.

It was 6.40 p.m. when the jury filed back into their seats and delivered a unanimous verdict of "Guilty".

Asked if he had anything to say before sentence of death was passed, Goozee stared at the judge and replied loudly: "I still state that I did not kill Norma Leakey."

The defendant then stood silent and ashen-faced, hands behind his back, flanked by four prison warders, as the judge's clerk placed the black square cap on the bewigged head of Mr Justice Havers. Following a new procedure adopted only a few months earlier, only the clerk and the High Sheriff's chaplain remained standing as Albert William Goozee was sentenced to death.

A provisonal date was fixed for Goozee's execution, but his sentence was commuted by the Home Secretary to one of life imprisonment.

Thus ended the final chapter in the story of the landlady, the lodger and the landlady's daughter that had climaxed in the fatal picnic. Perhaps the two female members of the trio had had some premonition that their affair would end in death. In the pocket of a coat hanging in Lydia Leakey's wardrobe was discovered a form of will to be used "in the event of anything happening to me". And her daughter – who was found to be still a virgin at the time of her death – had told relatives: "Albert will kill us one day."

10

THE DINNER PARTY MASSACRE

The murders of the Cleaver family and Margaret Murphy in 1986

At 10 a.m. on Tuesday September 2, 1986, 78-year-old Eddie Stubbings walked into Fordingbridge police station and announced simply: "I want to report a murder."

It was such a startling statement that for a moment PC Roger Carter was not sure whether to take it seriously.

"My first reaction was one of surprise," he recalled later. "It's the sort of comment you expect from someone coming to the counter and cracking a joke. I asked him to clarify what had happened. He was obviously in a state of shock. He said there was a woman who looked as if she had been strangled."

PC Carter and his colleague WPC Jan Bulfield arrived at Burgate House, home of retired publisher Joseph Cleaver and his wheelchair-bound wife, Hilda, within minutes, having driven there in separate cars. Eddie Stubbings, who worked as a gardener for the Cleavers, followed in a third car with his passenger, Mrs Nellie Taylor, who did domestic work at the rambling mansion overlooking the River Avon. Mrs Taylor had known the occupants for almost fifty years. The front door of the house was open and the two officers went inside. As they entered the hallway, they saw the Cleavers' pet poodle, Tina, whimpering in her basket. She had been clubbed and badly beaten; her jaw was broken and one eye was almost hanging out. Before the day was out, she would have been humanely destroyed by the R.S.P.C.A. Two other dogs, daschunds owned by Mr and Mrs Cleaver's son, Thomas, and his wife, Wendy, had fared less badly. They were obviously terrified, and rushing madly about the house, but were otherwise unharmed.

As PC Carter and WPC Bulfield moved tentatively forward, they noticed firelighters scattered around the floor and on the staircase. In places the red and blue carpeting was blackened and burned. They went upstairs. The door of the master bedroom was propped open by a jewellery box and smoke was billowing out. The officers were already expecting to find something horrific but the sight that confronted them was worse than they could have imagined.

"I could see one body sitting in a chair," PC Carter said in a subsequent interview with the *Bournemouth Evening Echo*. "The body had injuries to the head and I thought at first it was a man because she was wearing trousers. Lying in the middle of the bed was Mr Cleaver and there was another badly burnt body down by the side of the bed. There was still a lot of smoke in the room. It was just hanging there. A couple of fires were still burning. The bed and one of the chairs were still on fire."

PC Carter asked his female colleague to go outside and prevent anyone else entering the house. While WPC Bulfield radioed details of the discoveries to the Hampshire Police control room at Winchester, PC Carter asked Eddie Stubbings to lead him to the room where he had seen a woman's body. They found her in another bedroom. She was lying on her back, hands tied behind her, naked apart from a slip. Around her neck was tied a black ribbon. It was also clear that she had been set alight. Cautiously, PC Carter went over and touched the woman's arm. Rigor mortis had set in.

By this time, in response to the information relayed back by WPC Bulfield, other emergency vehicles were on their way to the scene. A Hampshire Fire Brigade crew were among the first to arrive and three firemen were allowed inside to put out the fires still smouldering in various parts of the building. Under the washbasin in an upstairs bathroom, one of the firemen made another gruesome discovery. It was a fifth body, that of a man with an artificial leg.

Soon large numbers of police officers were descending on Burgate House, among them some of the most senior detectives in the Hampshire force and a team of forensic experts. WPC Bulfield set up a control centre in the cottage adjoining Burgate House, recently vacated by the Cleavers' gardener-handyman George Stephenson and his wife, Fiona, whose short marriage had broken up. PC Carter went off to man the entrance gate the Cleavers shared with their nearest neighbours, the Game Conservancy. For several hours he chatted to the growing band of reporters arriving from the local and national media without disclosing the extent of his personal knowledge of the tragic discoveries 200 yards or so up the drive. The first journalists to arrive thought they were attending a fatal fire; they had no idea that they were at the scene of a multiple murder.

Meanwhile, in Burgate House itself, detectives were trying to piece together the last hours and minutes in the lives of Joe and Hilda Cleaver and their guests. It was already clear that the five victims were at dinner when they were interrupted by their killers. In the ground floor dining room, where pictures of the Prince and Princess of Wales and their children looked down from the wall, the table was set for a three-course meal, of which the first and main courses had evidently been eaten. It appeared that the intruders had ordered the diners away from the table and forced them to go upstairs. Four had then been herded into the master bedroom and tied up; a fifth was taken to another room. This was 46-year-old Wendy Cleaver, who had been tied up and gagged with part of a torn-up sheet, raped, and strangled with a length of black ribbon. Police found bruises on her body and bloodstains on the bedding.

Wendy Cleaver was dead before her body was set on fire and at first police believed that the three whose bodies were found in the master bedroom had suffered a similar fate. But later tests suggested they were still alive when the killers doused them with petrol, then threw lighted firelighters into the room. Joseph and Hilda Cleaver, both aged 82, and Mrs Cleaver's 70-year-old live-in nurse Margaret Murphy were all horrifically engulfed by a fire so fierce that the bed in the room had collapsed and was recognizable only by its springs. All three bodies were burned beyond recognition.

Four victims had been taken to the bedroom, but only three bodies were found there. Before the fire reached its height, 47-year-old Thomas Cleaver was able to use his artificial leg to break the twine that bound his ankles. Leaving a trail of skin on the carpet behind him, he managed to drag himself out of the bedroom and into an adjoining bathroom where, his hands still bound, he succeeded in smashing a window with his head in a desperate attempt to obtain fresh air and save himself. But beyond that, his efforts were in vain, and he slumped to an agonizing death beneath the washbasin where, more than twelve hours later, his body was found by a fireman. The head of Hampshire CID, Detective Chief Superintendent Alan Wheeler, was not exaggerating when, at a press conference on the afternoon of September 2, he described the killings as "very vicious and very brutal − murder as bad as you are likely to find".

Above: Burgate House on the day the murders were discovered. *(Photo: Bournemouth Evening Echo)*

Below: Detectives and forensic officers at Burgate House. *(Photo: Bournemouth Evening Echo)*

DCS Wheeler said the tragedy had "all the hallmarks of an interrupted burglary". Much of the house had been searched and it appeared that pictures had been moved in an attempt to find a wall safe hidden behind one of them. A colour television set and a video recorder were missing, along with two twelve-bore shotguns, a 410 shotgun and a .22 rifle. But the killers – and there must have been two or more – had failed to find £700 in cash that Tom Cleaver had kept hidden in his artificial leg.

Next morning, Fordingbridge found itself on the front page of every national newspaper as the Burgate House killings made massive headlines.

"DINNER TABLE MASSACRE: Five die in Britain's most horrific mass murder," screamed the *Star*.

"THE HOUSE OF HORROR: Charred bodies found in mansion," said *Today*.

All the reports described Joseph Cleaver as "wealthy"; some said he was a millionaire. He was, in fact, a founder and director of the Cleaver Hume Press, a publishing company specializing in educational correspondence courses, which he had built up with his partner Harry Hume. The family, including Tom Cleaver and his brother Jimmy, also ran the British Self Study Centre, together with a partner who lived at Fordingbridge. Joseph and Hilda were also well-known in the horse and greyhound racing fraternities. In the 1930s and '40s, they had their own string of racehorses, including two – Some Chicken and Sen Toi – that ran in the 1948 Grand National. A decade earlier, two of Joseph Cleaver's dogs, Juvenile Classic and Bay Moon, had come first and second in record time in the 1938 greyhound Grand National at the White City Stadium. Tom Cleaver, who had his own catering and wine bar business as well as an involvement in his father's company, had also inherited Joseph's love of racing. He and Wendy had their own house at Oxshott, Surrey, and also a flat at Cheltenham, home of the famous Cheltenham Gold Cup. In the three weeks before their deaths, Wendy had been staying with her husband's parents pending the arrival of replacements for the family's sacked handyman and housekeeper George and Fiona Stephenson.

By the time the national newspapers went to press with their first stories about the discoveries at Burgate House, Hampshire Police were already following up a lead that was to prove of crucial importance in the major murder investigation now underway. Watching early news of the killings on television in a London hotel room on the evening of September 2 was Fiona Stephenson, who had checked in in her maiden name of Clarke after leaving her husband. What she saw prompted her to go straight to Scotland Yard. And what she said there prompted Scotland Yard to contact Hampshire Police without delay.

Fiona told detectives of the two-week whirlwind romance with George Stephenson, the 36-year-old son of a sergeant major, that had led to their register-office wedding on September 6, 1985. George had been married once before, at the age of twenty, but that marriage had lasted only four years and since then he had earned himself a reputation as a ladies' man. According to her friends, Fiona was enchanted by Stephenson and remained so even when they split up on two occasions during their first few months of marriage. On both occasions they got back together and in July 1986 they left their home in London and went to stay with friends in the Moordown district of Bournemouth. While there they saw an advertisement in the *Evening Echo* for a "homely couple required for happy home in Fordingbridge". They decided to apply for the posts of handyman and housekeeper to the Cleavers and soon afterwards moved into a two-bedroom cottage in the grounds of Burgate House.

Not long after their arrival, Fiona told police, Stephenson began to beat her. They were in only their second week at Burgate when Joseph Cleaver asked Hannah Hunter, who was employed as relief nurse on Miss Murphy's days off, to look at an eye injury Fiona had sustained. "Mr Cleaver said that she had fallen and cut her eye," the relief nurse recalled later. "I always kept a bottle of witchhazel but the injury was so bad and in such a place that I couldn't imagine how she came to do it. I thought that her husband had hit her but I didn't pursue it."

On another occasion, the alarm bell from the servants' cottage suddenly rang out in Burgate House in the middle of the night. Then Fiona Stephenson appeared, saying her husband had come home drunk and there had been a violent row. The young housekeeper spent the rest of that night in a chair in Miss Murphy's room. Next day she hid in the garden shed before announcing that she was leaving her husband and did not want anyone to know where she was going. Joseph and Hilda Cleaver were greatly upset by the episode and on August 7, the Stephensons were sacked. The following day Stephenson returned. According to Hannah Hunter, he "looked wild and smelled of alcohol". He asked to see Joseph Cleaver and told him he had never done anything like that before and had never previously hit his wife. Then he asked his former employer for money, saying that Fiona had taken all their money with her when she left.

Police acted swiftly following their interview with Fiona Stephenson. Early on the morning of Wednesday September 3, a team of armed officers descended on the house in Moordown, Bournemouth, where the couple had stayed before obtaining their jobs at Fordingbridge. There they learned that Stephenson had come to the house at 7 p.m. on Monday evening and asked his friends if they wanted a television set. Next morning he had telephoned them, long distance, to check that they had got the set. Detectives eagerly examined the television, which had been left outside the house overnight. The officers quickly confirmed that it was the one missing from Burgate House. They also learned that during his visit, Stephenson had shown off his "new car" – a red C-registered Rover.

Later on Wednesday morning, police held a second press conference at Lyndhurst police station. There they issued copies of a photograph of George Stephenson taken on the day of his marriage to Fiona a year before. They also issued a description of the blue-eyed, brown-haired former handyman and of the red Rover car he had been driving in Bournemouth.

"Stephenson is described as a dangerous and violent man," Detective Chief Superintendent Wheeler told reporters. "It is for that reason that we have released his name. We think he is the key to this investigation. I would stress that members of the public should not under any circumstances approach him but should contact any police station if they see him."

He added: "He could be anywhere. He had connections in Eastbourne, Newhaven, Coventry and Bournemouth and he is from County Durham."

By Wednesday lunchtime, Stephenson's moustachioed face had appeared in evening newspapers and on television screens all over Britain. Almost immediately the publicity produced another vital lead. During the afternoon, Parkside Motors in Coventry telephoned the police to say that they had hired out a red Rover 213 to three men on Monday. It had been paid for by a cheque signed by a G. Daly and returned to the company's premises on Tuesday.

That evening, another set of dramatic front pages rolled off the presses of Fleet Street. None was more dramatic than that of the *Today* newspaper, which used a blown-up picture of Stephenson as the focal point of a full page "Wanted" poster. But even before the first editions hit the streets, Stephenson himself was heading out of Coventry on a train bound for Hampshire, a copy of that day's evening newspaper tucked under his arm. He left the train at Brockenhurst and went for a drink and a game of pool at the Foresters Arms. It was there that nurse Frances Marlow, who was on a New Forest camping holiday with her friend and colleague Georgia Farrow, picked up a copy of the *Coventry Evening Telegraph* and saw the picture of a man with a moustache wanted in connection with the Burgate House massacre. It was the first time she had heard or seen any news for

The Cleaver family's dinner table and the remains of the unfinished meal. *(Picture by courtesy of Hampshire Chief Constable)*

several days and the first she knew of the tragedy. But she did not connect the picture in the paper with the clean-shaven customer who was sitting nearby.

"I called him over because he was sitting on his own," Frances Marlow, an administrative sister at Stoke Mandeville Hospital, recalled later. "He said his name was Ray. He seemed very nervous, very uptight about something. I held his hand and started reading his palm. I asked him if anything was worrying him and he said he had been set up for something and had to go to Lyndhurst to sort it out. He would not say what it was and we had a guessing game mentioning murder, rape and robbery. When we left the pub at 11 p.m., he asked for a lift to Lyndhurst, but we said it was too far. We took him back to our camp-site, where he was going to phone for a taxi."

At the Roundhill campsite, the trio drank wine together and shared a cannabis cigarette provided, according to the girls, by Stephenson. The guessing game was resumed and Stephenson asked Frances if she had read the newspaper properly. She remembered the article on the front page and asked: "Are you George Stephenson, by any chance?" He replied that he was and produced a driving licence bearing his name. Frances asked if he had done the murders and he repeatedly said he had not. He told them he had set up a robbery at Burgate House for two Hell's Angels called Lynne and Gary. His share was to have been a television and video recorder.

"He said he did not expect them to go through with it," Frances Marlow recalled. Then he turned to her and said: "For Christ's sake, they killed nice people, harmless people."

Before he left, Frances Marlow asked Stephenson to autograph the newspaper photograph for her, which he did. Then, lighting his way with a borrowed candle, he found his way to the camp-site telephone box, dialled 999, and told police: "My name is George Stephenson. I've seen myself on the television regarding those murders. I'm on my way to your station. I'll be there in about two hours."

In fact, Stephenson was not required to make his own way to Lyndhurst. The police were only too happy to give him a lift. He was still talking to them from the campsite callbox at 2 a.m. when two uniformed officers arrived to arrest him. At about the same time, 25-year-old George Daly, who had signed the cheque for the hire of the Rover, was arrested in Coventry following an operation involving thirty officers. A few hours later, his 21-year-old brother, John, was also arrested by armed police officers as he walked down a Coventry street. All three were taken to Winchester's North Walls police station, which had a specially equipped room where interviews could be tape-recorded.

There was tight security on Saturday September 6, when the three men made their first court appearances at Lymington. Each was dealt with separately and applications for them to be detained for further questioning under the new Police and Criminal Evidence Act were granted by the magistrates.

That same Saturday was the day on which the people of Fordingbridge were due to stage their Domesday 900 festival and carnival to commemorate the 900th anniversary of the town's Domesday Book roots. Inevitably, the recent events at Burgate House cast a shadow over the festivities but they went ahead more or less as planned, with special prayers being said at St Mary's Church. "It was important to continue with the festival – it proves that life goes on after the most horrendous event in the town's history," the Vicar of St Mary's, the Rev. Roger Stirrup, told the *Evening Echo*. "It's a cathartic release of pent-up sadness. It heals and restores the town after a week of national attention."

George Francis Stephenson, George Anthony Daly and John Joseph Daly made their first public court appearances on Monday September 8, again at Lymington. All three faced five charges of murder and were remanded in custody for seven days. In fact, they remained in custody for eleven months before their trial opened at Winchester Crown Court. By then, all three had also been charged with raping Wendy Cleaver and with robbing Joseph Cleaver of three shotguns, two air rifles, a quantity of ammunition, a television set, a video recorder, a watch, and a quantity of alcohol and jewellery; Stephenson was also accused of aiding and abetting, counselling and procuring both George and John Daly to rape Wendy Cleaver, although these two charges were later withdrawn by the Judge, the Hon Mr Justice Hobhouse.

The trial opened on October 5, 1987, and attracted world-wide media interest. Forty-two press, television and radio journalists were present in the courtroom, those from Fleet Street and the American NBC network being accommodated on the usual Press benches, the remainder in reserved seats in the packed public gallery above. Stephenson and George Daly pleaded not guilty to all charges; John Daly pleaded not guilty to the five murder charges. But it was only when Mr David Elfer, QC, began to outline the case for the prosecution that the full horror of the circumstances surrounding the dinner party massacre began to emerge.

Mr Elfer said the four members of the Cleaver family and Miss Murphy were about to begin their sweet course at the dinner table when three men, wearing stocking masks and rubber gloves, burst in. They were armed with pickaxe handles, though later one of them armed himself with a loaded gun taken from the house. They had also brought with them two one-gallon cans of petrol, firelighters and some string.

"The plan of these three men was to rob the Cleaver household. They were there for money, they were there for guns and ammunition," Mr Elfer told the court. "They were there to steal a video and television; they were there to steal any jewellery and other valuable items they could find. But the plan went further. No-one was going to live to tell the tale. The house was going to be burnt to the ground, covering all the clues of what happened that night."

But, Mr Elfer continued, the plan went wrong. For although petrol was poured on four of the victims and the building set alight, Burgate House did not collapse or go up in flames as the men had anticipated.

"They were not to realise that it was made entirely of concrete and, instead of catching fire, the blaze confined itself to the one room and so, the following morning, the grisly truth was revealed. The men had a rude awakening on September 3 when they switched on the television and were confronted with news of the incident. On the television screen was a picture of Burgate House still standing, a picture of Stephenson and the words: 'We're looking for this man'."

Mr Elfer said Joseph Cleaver suffered from a bad heart, Hilda had been a wheelchair-bound invalid since suffering a stroke some years before and Thomas Cleaver had an artificial leg. All except Hilda Cleaver were tied up.

It was at this point that Thomas and Wendy Cleaver's 21-year-old son Jason tried to telephone the house. His first call went unanswered. His second was answered.

"Fordingbridge," said a man's voice.

Jason asked to speak to his father.

"He's upstairs," said the voice.

Jason wanted to leave a message, but the phone was hung up. He rang a third time and asked to speak to his mother.

"Don't be stupid, she can't speak," said the same voice.

Jason left another message asking his father to call him back. Minutes later, Thomas Cleaver did just that, having been untied by the raiders and taken to the telephone.

"They took that very brave man downstairs to ring up Jason to prove that all was well at Burgate House, and that mum had merely got 'flu and was upstairs and that there was nothing to worry about," said Mr Elfer. "The telephone wires were then pulled out."

It was shortly after this, said the prosecution counsel, that Stephenson dragged Wendy Cleaver into another room, where she was savagely abused before being killed. When found by police, her hands were still tied behind her back but the gag had been removed to slip down on to her chin.

"Her clothes had been unceremoniously torn from her private parts," said Mr Elfer. "It was evident that sexual intercourse had been had with her, and violent sexual intercourse at that. Petrol had been poured on her, too, although she was dead by the time that happened. She, too, had to go in the conflagration —

The *Today* newspaper's dramatic front page on September 4 took the form of a "Wanted" poster. *(Picture by kind permission of Today newspaper)*

The people rince Charles trusts

CENTRE PAGES

TODAY

THURSDAY, SEPTEMBER 4, 1986   20p

Fordingbridge Everybody's nightmare

PAGE 6

George Stephenson, age 35, height 5ft. 9in., blue eyes, brown hair, neat moustache. Dangerous and violent. Do not approach. Contact police.

WANTED

Massacre at Fordingbridge - Page 2

otherwise too many clues would be available."

Some members of the jury turned pale and two women asked for glasses of water as Mr Elfer told them how John Daly had described Wendy Cleaver's death to the police.

"He described how he turned her on to her face and pulled the cord tight around her neck until her face turned blue," said Mr Elfer.

He added: "The fact that Wendy was raped in such a disgusting fashion and then strangled shows that no-one was going to come out alive. That is why they could toy with other human beings in such a way."

For all this, Mr Elfer told the jury, the raiders had netted just £90 between them.

Early witnesses for the prosecution included Edgar Stubbings and Nellie Taylor, who described how they found Wendy Cleaver's body, and pathologist Dr Roger Ainsworth, who said it would have taken at least half-a-minute for Wendy to die of strangulation. Forensic scientist Dr Rodney May said the fire that had engulfed the master bedroom had involved a "very explosive force" – ornaments from the room were found outside, having been pushed through the windows as the curtains billowed out like a ship's sails. He said the explosion would have been accompanied by a "whoosh" sound and would have rapidly used up the oxygen in the room.

George Daly's common-law wife, Ruth Smith, a widow and mother of three children, including one fathered by Daly, also gave evidence, and at one point broke down sobbing. She told the court that Stephenson stayed with them after leaving his job at Fordingbridge. She had ironed clothes for the two men to wear on their day trip to the south, the purpose of which, she was told, was for Stephenson to pick up some clothes and drink and to see some people in Bournemouth. At 3 a.m. on September 2, she was woken by the sounds of partying and went downstairs to find George and John Daly and Stephenson drinking and listening to music. There were bottles of gin, whisky, vodka and wine on the table and John Daly looked very drunk and had his head down. The following night, over a curry meal, she asked George why he was quiet and moody and he replied: "If only you knew what I have been doing." Later that night, four guns and some ammunition were brought into the house from the garage. Mrs Smith said she was watching television with a friend, Paula Harrison, when details of the killings and Stephenson's picture appeared on the screen. When Stephenson returned, Paula, who had turned down an invitation from Stephenson to go on the trip, told him: "You're a vicious, dangerous man," to which he replied: "Do I look like a vicious, dangerous man?" Then he said he was going to give himself up.

Detective Chief Inspector Dennis Luty told the court that following the arrests, he visited Stephenson in his cell and broke the news to him that his wife, Fiona, had tried to commit suicide by taking an overdose of drugs. Stephenson then admitted for the first time that he had been to Burgate House on the night of the robbery but claimed that he had sat in the car while the Daly brothers were in the mansion. However, the court also heard that Stephenson hotly denied having this conversation with Mr Luty.

Tape recordings of interviews with each of the defendants played a prominent role in the trial. In one recording, Stephenson repeated to police the story which he had told to the girl campers at Brockenhurst – that he talked about Burgate House to two hitchhikers he picked up while driving alone to Bournemouth and that they said they intended to rob the place. Stephenson also told police: "The Cleavers were a very nice old couple and it is awful what has happened to them. I just want to clear my name. I can swear to God I have no blood on my hands. I have not killed nobody, I have burned nobody, I have killed no animal."

At one point, Detective Chief Inspector Luty was heard to tell Stephenson: "I'll say this for George and John: they have both fallen apart, their conscience has been pricked. They are very remorseful for what they have done. But you – nothing."

In his recorded interview, George Daly admitted going to Burgate House and described what happened when he entered the dining room. He said people were eating and he was telling them to be quiet and sit down and have their meal and everything would be all right. His little brother, John, was also there, and then Stephenson came in with a shotgun in his hand. Later, said George in the taped interview, he went into a bedroom and saw Stephenson having intercourse with the youngest of the three women, who was bound and gagged. He fled the room immediately but minutes later Stephenson emerged with a loaded shotgun and said that all three must rape the woman. He said that he then got on the bed with Mrs Cleaver but could not make love to her properly.

"I felt sick and felt as if I was going to throw up," he said.

Asked why he raped Wendy Cleaver, he said he did so because Stephenson had a loaded shotgun. When he left her, she was still alive. Then his brother disappeared with Stephenson, to reappear some time later in tears.

"I've never seen him look like that. It wasn't John I was looking at. It was my brother, but it wasn't," he said.

During the interview, Daly broke down, muttering: "No-one should have got hurt."

He said that when they went to the house, he thought that they were going only to steal things and would leave the occupants in one piece. But he admitted lighting a firelighter and throwing it into the bedroom in which Stephenson had previously poured petrol over the four people.

"I was very frightened – it freaked me out," he said in the interview. "I lit a firelighter and it burnt my hand so I dropped it. I picked it up, lit it again and threw it into the bedroom where the four people were. But I thought they were dead. It just went up in a big flash." He broke down, sobbing, as he told detectives: "I thought they were dead, otherwise I wouldn't have done it. He [Stephenson] told me they were fucking dead." He wept again in the dock as the interview was played.

The jury also heard a tearful John Daly say, again in recorded interviews, that Stephenson had mentioned the Burgate House family and had said that he would "pop them all off". But Daly did not agree with the plan and did not think he would have to kill anyone. Between sobs, he also said to detectives: "They'll put me away for fucking life."

John Daly said he spent about ten minutes with Wendy Cleaver and while he was raping her, Stephenson came in with a knife and a piece of cloth ribbon.

"I knew what they were for – to kill her with," he said.

He then described how he turned Wendy Cleaver on to her stomach so that he did not have to see her face while he strangled her. Her body fell off the bed and when he had finished tying the ligature, he picked her up and put her back on the bed. He then went downstairs, where he cried and was comforted by Stephenson. He said he felt sick and left the house to go and sit in the back of the car.

It was on October 15, ten days after the trial opened, that George Francis Stephenson stepped into the witness box at Winchester Crown Court to state that he played no part in the Burgate House massacre. He said he drove there at George Daly's request and was "astounded" when, having got out of the car, the two brothers reappeared wearing masks and rubber gloves and armed with sticks. He said he asked them "what the fucking hell" they thought they were doing and George Daly replied: "I want the guns and as we are here I'm going to get them."

"I said: 'You're fucking crazy. You're out of order,'" Stephenson told the court. "It was a silly idea. It was was stupid to even consider it."

He said George Daly reached into the car to grab the ignition keys and told him not to worry but to sit tight. Then he disappeared and returned minutes later brandishing a shotgun.

"I said: 'You're going to get me into a lot of trouble. You really are crazy.' He was laughing and seemed to think it was funny that I was protesting about us being there. He seemed to think that he had it all under control. He laughed and went back into the house. Both of them came back with a TV and a video."

It was Stephenson's own defence counsel, Mr Brian Escott-Cox, who first told the court that the former Burgate House handyman had "quite a substantial criminal record", including a conviction for possessing a firearm. Cross-examined by Mr Anthony Palmer, Q.C., for George Daly, Stephenson agreed there were forty-six different offences recorded against him but denied that he was an habitual criminal or that he had no conscience. He told the court: "I am not a man of violence. I have not gone around strangling people."

To Mr Rock Tansey, Q.C., for John Daly, Stephenson added: "Your client is the man who done the evil, and his brother."

John Daly did not give evidence in the trial but his brother told from the witness box how, before going to Burgate House, Stephenson took them to Poole to see the scene of another robbery he said he had been involved in. The purpose of the trip was "to show us he'd done one before and boost our confidence for the tie-up", said George Daly. He also repeated his claim that he believed the other four victims were already dead when he threw a firelighter into the master bedroom, and said he wished that when Stephenson ordered them to rape Wendy Cleaver, he had taken the shotgun off him and shot him.

"I have got nothing against George Stephenson. I have got no reason to involve him if he did not take part, but he did," said George Daly. "He was the ringleader. I'm not going to get off. I'm going to get locked up because of my involvement. I'm not daft enough to think I am going to walk away from this court. Mr Stephenson thinks he will."

George Daly described his "baby brother" as a very shy man, who rarely mixed with friends or went out with girls and who suffered from a "voice blockage" when embarrassed. His hobbies were painting and playing the guitar but he never expressed his wants or feelings and "you wouldn't get him to use a telephone".

But of Stephenson, he said: "He's overpowering. He can manipulate, to do what he wants. He's always come on as though he's very outward going and always done a lot. Bragging is the word. On that night, he was confident and in charge. He was content with what he was doing."

It was 11.03 a.m. on October 27 when the jury of eight men and four women retired to consider their verdicts in the Burgate House trial. Five-and-a-half hours later, recalled by the judge, the foreman announced that they had found both George Daly and George Stephenson guilty of robbery and rape – charges to which John Daly had already pleaded guilty. But they had been unable to reach agreement on the murder charges.

"What?" gasped Stephenson as the guilty verdicts on him were announced. He shook his head in disbelief but the Daly brothers stared straight ahead.

After a night in an hotel, the jury resumed their task and returned to the court following a total of nine hours' deliberation. Then they presented the court with a remarkable set of verdicts. John Daly, the youngest of the trio, who claimed to have played no direct part in the killing of the four people burnt to death, was found guilty of all five murders, four of them by a majority of 11-1, that of Wendy Cleaver unanimously. George Stephenson, who denied entering the house but was described by the prosecution as the ringleader, was found not guilty of murdering Wendy Cleaver but guilty of the other four murders. George Daly, who said he threw a firelighter into the master bedroom believing the people inside were already dead, was found not guilty of all five murders but guilty of the manslaughter of all except Wendy Cleaver.

It was a set of verdicts that made little sense to anyone apart, presumably, from the jurors themselves. It was riddled with inconsistencies, the most glaring of which was that while the man who threw the firelighter which led to the deaths of four people had not been found guilty of any of the murders, his timid younger brother, who, according to the evidence, was directly involved only in the death of Wendy Cleaver, was convicted on five counts of murder.

To some extent, the sentences handed out by Mr Justice Hobhouse corrected the inconsistencies. Stephenson was given six life sentences with a recommendation that he serve a minimum of twenty-five years. The judge told him: "These murders were committed in circumstances of indescribable barbarity. You were the leader in all that occurred that night. You showed no mercy and you deserve none. In view of the gravity of the crimes, I consider I should make a recommendation of imprisonment for twenty-five years."

Part of the eight-page background supplement published by the *Evening Echo*, Bournemouth, at the end of the Burgate House trial. It includes pictures of Stephenson and the Daly brothers and of their five victims. *(Picture by kind permission of Bournemouth Evening Echo)*

The House of Horror

An Echo exclusive report by Pat Fleming

George Stephenson — 25 years.

George Daly — 22 years.

John Daly — Life.

Thomas Cleaver

Wendy Cleaver

Hilda Cleaver

Joseph Cleaver

Margaret Murphy

Their last supper . . .

THIS is the table at which he victims of the Burgate House slaughter sat down to inner.

The first course and the main course had been eaten and all the signs show that the five were dragged from the table while they ate.

A bowl of green vegetables and melons brought to the house the previous day by local greengrocery worker Dan Lennan, lay on the neatly laid table.

Dan had brought broccoli, courgettes, carrots and a range of fruit which lay almost untouched in the fruit bowl.

A sharpened knife lay on a cloth to assist in the carving of the meat.

On the wall above the table were pictures of the Prince and Princess of Wales and their two children.

But this homely scene belied the savagery of the killings.

Millionaire Joseph Cleaver, his wife Hilda, son Thomas, daughter-in-law Wendy and live-in-nurse Margaret Murphy had been brutally slaughtered.

They were so badly burned that police had to mark the corpses A, B, C, D and E.

Three of the bodies in the master bedroom were eventually identified only through jewellery and dentures.

Body C was a female identified by a caliper fitted to one of her legs. This was Hilda Cleaver.

Body A, Margaret Murphy, was identified by corset wires.

Joseph Cleaver, Margaret Murphy, Hilda Cleaver and Tom Cleaver had all burned to death.

Petrol had been thrown over them as the four were held in the bedroom they had been herded into by the raiders.

Firelighters were then thrown into the petrol soaked room and the four were left to burn.

Tom Cleaver fought his way out of the room to the adjoining bathroom and it is thought that he made a desperate attempt to save himself by smashing the window.

His effort was in vain and he died.

His wife Wendy had been taken to a separate room tied and gagged and viciously raped by all three men.

Wendy had been subjected to awful abuse before she was strangled by a man less than half her age.

The killers showed no mercy either toward Joseph and Hilda Cleaver's pet poodle Tina.

She was clubbed and beaten and was found whimpering in her bed. Her jaw was broken and one eye was almost hanging out. She was later humanely destroyed by the RSPCA.

Tom and Wendy Cleaver's two dachshunds were found in the house suffering from the effects of smoke.

Hardened Hampshire policeman Chief Supt. Alan Wheeler emerged with his colleague Det. Chief Insp. Dennis Luty from the scene to describe it as "Killings as bad as you are likely to find."

"It was very vicious and very brutal," he said.

Scores of detectives were on the scene in hours searching every blade of grass outside for clues.

The red and blue carpeted floors downstairs and upstairs had been soaked with petrol.

Bits of firelighters were thrown all around the house.

Signs of robbery lay everywhere. Knives and been taken out of drawers, and an untidy search had been made, a half drunk bottle of milk stood by the front door.

A range of property had been taken but untouched were the paintings which stood on the wall above the ornate staircase leading to the upstairs rooms where the savage killings took place.

The entrance to the master bedroom indicated all was not well. The door had been wedged open with a jewel case.

Pieces of firelighter were strewn by the door and inside in the fire-blackened room lay three bodies.

Det. Insp. Dennis Luty

Photographs: by Echo photographer John Gilbride and Hampshire Police

Sentencing John Daly to life imprisonment for murder but with no additional recommendation, the judge told him: "You are the youngest member and it appears you are easily led. You have been more frank than the other two, pleading guilty to robbery and rape."

George Daly, sentenced to twenty-two years for manslaughter and sixteen years each for rape and robbery, was told that his acquittal on the murder charges showed that the jury were not satisfied that he ever intended anyone to be killed.

"However," the judge continued, "the gravity of the crimes remains extreme. Your reckless disregard for human life is shown in your own evidence."

So ended the trial of three men accused of crimes that many saw as being among the most horrific of modern times.

Most people who attended the trial in person were lawyers, police officers, reporters, witnesses, and others whose professions or connections with the case dictated their presence in the courtroom. But also present to hear every last harrowing detail were two young people who could, had they wished, have stayed away and spared themselves an even greater ordeal than they had already endured. The steadfast and dignified silence that Jason Cleaver and his 19-year-old sister, Melissa, had kept during the eleven months leading up to the trial was maintained throughout the hearing itself. Occasionally, they showed signs of emotion, as when they smiled faintly upon hearing the "guilty" verdicts, as when Melissa fought back tears as the rape and death of her mother were described. But always she and Jason and other surviving members of the family retained the dignity that was denied to Wendy Cleaver. It was a dignity that shone through even in their one public statement, made to the press immediately after the trial.

"The murder of our family last year dealt a tragic blow to those of us who remain," said the statement. "We could not even attempt to put into words the impact of this and the deep grief that this and the loss of our much loved family nurse has caused us all. It may be wondered why we, as a family, should have attended the trial and, to the outsider, seemingly inflicted even more pain on ourselves. Again it would be foolish to attempt to explain the reasons. How could the bystander be expected to understand? Suffice it to say that it has been necessary for us all to go through the trial process, to help each other and as a duty to those we have lost. Not knowing what happened during the evening of September 1, 1986, has been a heavy burden to bear. We have felt a great need actually to take part, albeit silently."

One person who was not present to hear the verdicts was Eddie Stubbings. It was he who had discovered Wendy Cleaver's body on September 2, 1986; it was he who headed the list of prosecution witnesses in October 1987. The tragedy and the trial preyed heavily on his mind and eventually proved too much for him. On October 23, as the trial neared the end of its third week, Mr Stubbings was found dead in a chair at his home in Ringwood.

Since the trial, the surviving members of the Cleaver family have, not surprisingly, had Burgate House razed to the ground and the site sold. Since the trial also, both George Stephenson and John Daly have appealed against their murder convictions, claiming that the jury was misdirected by the judge. Both appeals were dismissed by three judges at the Court of Appeal in London on May 11, 1990.

SOURCES

THE HUSBAND KILLERS

Western Circuit Jail Books (ASSI 23/6-10, Public Record Office)

A Full and True Account of a most Barbarous and Bloody Murther, committed by Esther Ives, with the assistance of John Noyse, a Cooper, on the Body of William Ives, her Husband, at Rumsey in Hampshire, on the Fifth day of February, 1686 (1686)

A True and Genuine Account of Lady Kirk, who was tried at the Assizes at Winchester in Hampshire and found Guilty of poisoning her husband, two sons and a daughter and received sentence of death, with a particular relation of her public execution etc. (c. 1760)

Guttridge, Roger, *Dorset Murders* (1986)

Hampshire Chronicle

Hampshire Notes and Queries, Volume II (1884), Volume IV (1889)

Lane, Brian (ed), *The Murder Club Guide to South-East England* (1988)

Moody, Henry, *Notes and Essays Relating to the Counties of Hants and Wilts* (1851)

THE DUELLIST IN THE DOCK

A List of all the Officers of the Army and Royal Marines on Full and Half-Pay (1795-1936)

Assize Court records (Public Record Office. ASSI 21/29 and 23/10)

Baldick, Robert, *The Duel: A History of Duelling* (1965)

Hampshire Chronicle (1814)

King, Edward, *Old Times Revisited in the Borough and Parish of Lymington, Hants* (1879, 1900)

Patterson, Moira, "The Duellist who was Tried for Murder" (*Hampshire the County Magazine*, 1961)

Trevelyan, G. M., *English Social History* (1944)

THE SON OF SATAN

Assize Court records (Public Record Office. ASSI 26/1)

Griffiths, Arthur, *The Chronicles of Newgate* (1883, 1987)

Hampshire Chronicle (1862)

Hoskins, John, "Poor Mary Dreamt of her Death" (*Southern Evening Echo* 1987)

Hoskins, John, "Son of Satan Trial Uproar" (*Southern Evening Echo* 1987)

HORROR IN THE HOP-GARDEN

Brewer's Dictionary of Phrase and Fable (1989)

Browne, John Paddy, *Folk Songs of Old Hampshire* (1987)

Hampshire Chronicle (1867-8, 1896)

Lane, Brian (ed), *The Murder Club Guide to South-East England* (1988)
Laurence, John, *A History of Capital Punishment* (1932)
West Surrey Times (1867)

THE COACHMAN'S CONQUEST
Hampshire Chronicle (1896)
Honeycombe, Gordon, *The Murders of the Black Museum* (1982)
Hoskins, John, "Three Killers Who Died at the Scaffold" (*Southern Evening Echo*
    1987)

THE POISONED PARTRIDGES
Aldershot Gazette and Military News (1931)
Daily Sketch (1931)
Glaister, John, *The Power of Poison* (1954)
Lane, Brian (ed), *The Murder Club Guide to South-East England* (1988)
Southern Daily Echo (1931)
Thompson, C. J. S. *Poison Mysteries Unsolved* (1937)

THE OLD LAG'S ALIBI
Browne, Douglas G., and Tullett, E.V., *Bernard Spilsbury: His Life and Cases* (1951)
Casswell, J. D., *A Lance for Liberty* (1961)
Evening News, Portsmouth (1943-44)

DEATH ON THE DURBAN CASTLE
Casswell, J. D., *A Lance for Liberty* (1961)
Roberts, G. D., *Law and Life* (1964)
Southern Daily Echo (1947-48, 1958-59, 1971)

THE FATAL PICNIC
Bournemouth Daily Echo, (1956)
Guttridge, Roger, *Dorset Murders* (1986)
Jones, Walter, *My Own Case* (1966)
Small, Don, and Chapman, John (eds), *Explore the New Forest: An official guide by the
    Forestry Commission* (1987)

THE DINNER PARTY MASSACRE
Daily Express (1986-87)
Daily Telegraph (1986-87)
Evening Echo, Bournemouth (1986-89)
The Mirror (1986-87)
The Star (1986-87)
Today (1986-87)
and the author's personal knowledge of the case

ACKNOWLEDGEMENTS

The author is grateful to all who have helped with the preparation of this book, in particular Bob Richardson, Kelly Way, Bernice Walkey, Nigel and Eileen Witt, Mrs C.E.C. Sykes, John Hoskins of the *Southern Evening Echo*, Brigadier John Woodroff, Lt Col Patric J Emerson, Major Alan Harfield and staff at the Public Record Office, British Library, British Library Newspaper Library, Bodleian Library, Hampshire County Library at Winchester and Portsmouth, Southampton University Library, Dorset County Library at Wimborne and the Lansdowne, Bournemouth.

Grateful acknowledgments are also due to Pat Fleming, Editor of the *Southern Evening Echo*; Gareth Weekes, Editor of the *Evening Echo*, Bournemouth; the Editor of *The News*, Portsmouth; the Editor of *Today*; the Chief Constable of Hampshire; the British Library Newspaper Library; and the Bodleian Library, Oxford, for permission to reproduce photographs.

INDEX